I AM the WHALE

I AM the WHALE

Daniel Miller

I AM THE WHALE

Daniel Miller

ISBN: 978-1-968149-24-6

Joint Venture Publishing
The Millionaire Mentor, Inc.

Printed in the United States of America

Praise for I Am the Whale

"Daniel Miller has painted an ethereal picture of a powerful and thought-provoking odyssey of the soul, with lyrical, symbolic, and deep human elements woven beautifully within. I Am the Whale is that book you'll never forget."

Dr. Remina Panjwani, Military Veteran, Best-selling Author Odd Girl Out, Doctor Within

"This story awakens the greatness already inside you."

Dr. Greg S. Reid, #1 Best-Selling author, founder of Secret Knock

Table of Contents

Dedication

For my loving parents,

Douglas and Susan Miller,

whose enduring support and quiet wisdom

offered the mirrors through which this story

was able to reveal itself.

Prologue

I once developed a theory there was no such thing as original thought. It came from noticing how often an idea that felt new to me had already been expressed by someone else. In time, I realized the concept itself was not unique to my mind. Mark Twain was known to have said, "There's no such thing as original thought," nearly a century before. That realization reinforced the idea, though it also carried a measure of disappointment. It felt as though something I had hoped to claim had already been taken, named, and set aside.

Raised in a religious tradition with a strong emphasis on prayer, I set out with all due fervor to ask the divine creator for the chance to experience something wholly my own. Over time, a simple conclusion surfaced and settled with humility: You are it.

Me. My body, my mind, and my soul.

It is all completely original. I am the embodiment of the very thing I was seeking outside myself. I am not my distant relative Mark Twain. I am a singular being, shaped by time, circumstance, and choice, connected to the world through an invisible and energetic bond that precedes lineage or language. That realization did not arrive as revelation so much as recognition. It became the ocean from which the whale dream later surfaced.

This is where the story begins, with a dream I experienced while asleep. It carried a clarity and emotional coherence that resisted being dismissed as imagination alone. It did not fade upon waking. Instead, it followed me into daylight and remained present, quietly insisting it mattered. I carried it with me through ordinary moments, noticing how it surfaced without warning, as if asking not to be forgotten.

Even with its weight and emotional resonance, I did not feel as if I was particularly spiritual, mystical, or endowed with any special gifts. I was, after all, just a man living a normal life, informed by service, responsibility, and reflection. Yet this whale dream, explored in the first three chapters, came with a gravity I had never experienced before. It felt transported from somewhere else, whether from my subconscious or from a shared field of meaning beyond it. When I awoke that spring morning in 2024, the sensation lingered in my body before it reached my thoughts. I remember lying still, listening to my breath, unsure whether I had returned fully. Like Jonah, I found myself inside the whale while trying to understand the message.

I did not know why it appeared. I only knew that it altered how I understood my life and place in the world. I felt drawn to share it, whether for my own understanding or for others who might recognize something of themselves in it. Perhaps both. I chose to tell the story because it felt too alive to keep to myself. In doing so, I suspected I would not be alone. Many people carry dreams that linger and ask to be remembered. I will also admit to another reason for telling it. By laying the story out in words, I hoped to find my own answers.

From there, the work became quieter and more deliberate. One idea surfaced early and stayed with me. There is something singular about the whale's breath. Whales are masters of it. Their capacity far exceeds that of humans, allowing them to descend into depths that feel like another world entirely. Prior to my dream that night, I had been working diligently on breathing and meditation, and it was proving to have a calming and centering effect on me. The dream seemed to arise from a deeper register of awareness, one I felt connected to through that practice.

Many of the journal notes that became part of this book emerged through recall during long meditative sessions. I remembered details clearly, yet my mind remained open to meaning beyond memory alone. The dream felt layered, offering more than one point of entry. I could not tell whether its messages were meant to be grasped directly, but my curiosity would not allow me to ignore them. When time permitted, I recorded the dream itself and my attempts to understand its origin and purpose.

Like many who have lived through trauma, I searched for meaning. I reflected on the paths I had taken and the reasons I might have landed in this body. I felt called to serve and wanted to be part of a force for good. I felt balanced in life, yet I continued to seek meaning and growth. At the time of the whale dream, I had no idea it would lead me to share these experiences with others. Over time, I came to believe that what is given should be shared. I could not deny that this dream felt like one of the most original gifts I had received, arriving without warning.

Only later did I realize how naturally these threads of service, trauma, dream, and story began to gather. What felt novel was the weaving together of lived experience, an inspired dream, and the enduring themes of classic literature. Prior to beginning this writing process, I had never read Herman Melville's Moby-Dick. I was unfamiliar with its characters or its deeper meanings. And yet, as I encountered it, the story felt like an unexpected mirror. Its questions of obsession, witness, suffering, and the cost of human arrogance aligned naturally with the moral inquiries already unfolding within me. The dream and Melville's story were speaking to the same symbolic language.

For much of my life, I would have considered myself uncultured in literature, as it never held my attention. Yet through this imaginative writing process, I came to see how a classic work like Moby-Dick can serve as a vessel for meaning, particularly one capable of carrying lived experience, memory, and inquiry into a newly revealed world. After reading Melville's classic story, I was drawn to Ishmael and his longing for adventure. His journey mirrored something I recognized in myself. By placing my own experiences in loose conversation with Melville's story, I discovered a creative and purposeful way to explore the questions of my own life, specifically those shaped by trauma and the long work of healing after military service.

This approach allowed me to honor my ancestry, both mortal and unseen, while keeping the story inclusive and non-sectarian. Readers are invited to encounter the work through their own sense of meaning and interpretation. In the end, this story feels original because it stands on its own and because it was born from an honest inner place. It is offered in that spirit. In that way, it quietly challenges the belief that first set this journey in motion, that there is no such thing as an original thought.

Chapter One

"The Awakening"

I awaken from darkness into a heavy velvet world of silence. Slowly, my eyes adjust to my surroundings, catching a faint glimmer of light up ahead. I move toward it, diving deeper even as my body accelerates forward, returning to a place my movements seem to remember, though no word for it rises within me.

Water glides off my body as I move, responding instantly to each shift in form and direction. Something settles in me as I dive deeper and move faster, a sense of return carried in motion rather than thought. The water answers me as if it has known me all along, even as a quiet difference hums beneath the familiarity.

Movement requires no effort. The water carries me as much as I carry myself. It accommodates my acceleration and direction with just enough friction for my muscles to navigate further and change paths. Power moves through my body in slow, deliberate waves, distributed and steady, allowing the density around me to yield rather than oppose. Pressure becomes guidance, and motion unfolds without strain. I feel at home within this motion. Calm and natural, it is accompanied by a subtle sense of weightlessness.

The depths stretch outward and downward around me, swallowing distance until there is no clear boundary to measure against. As I move through them, my body feels simultaneously vast and contained, carried within a space that does not acknowledge edges.

Other inhabitants pass nearby, their movements quick and bright against the surrounding dark. As I approach, they alter their paths, widening their arcs without panic or hesitation. Space opens around me. Their behavior registers before meaning does, and only afterward do I sense the quiet acknowledgment of my presence and force.

Awareness turns inward. I begin to feel every part of my body at once. Pressure prickles across my skin, spreading in a wide circumference as though countless points of sensation are awakening together. Each one traces the outline of my form, defining my girth and scale from the outside in.

Something within this awareness does not settle cleanly. Sensation carries more than instinct alone. A subtle tension hums beneath it, layered and unresolved, as if more than one way of knowing is moving through me at the same time.

Who am I?

What am I?

Where did I come from?

Why am I here?

The questions ripple through me, and with them a name stirs, faint but insistent, brushing the edges of my consciousness.

Ishmael.

The name resonates, pulling memories from a lifetime left behind. Images flash without order. A wooden ship tossed in a storm. Rope and sails strained by wind. A captain consumed by resentment and vengeance. The great white whale. Awareness gathers around the Pequod, around Ahab, around the chaos and the loss that followed. The impressions are faint but insistent, arriving as fragments rather than lived experience. That consciousness moves within me now, inhabiting this body and lending it the weight of reflection, the ache of survival, and a strange, persistent yearning to understand.

Playful swimming and instinctive songs move through the forefront of my awareness, while Ishmael's essence flows within me. His memories fold into mine like tides blending with the ocean, carrying stories of obsession, tragedy, and the cost of unchecked longing. Together, we exist as both predator and witness, creature and chronicler.

Have I been here before? I am not certain, yet a deep connection persists as my awareness shifts between form and formlessness. One state feels vast and unbounded, familiar in a way that resists memory. The other gathers around weight, movement, and breath.

The distant realm lingers only briefly now, its presence softening as it begins to recede from awareness. The transition feels gradual, like returning from a powerful dream into the steady familiarity of a body.

Awareness settles. The formless loosens its hold, and consciousness drifts fully into the living presence of the whale I have become.

Uncertainty lingers briefly, suspended between dreaming and waking, before beginning to dissolve. Calm gathers steadily, settling through me as the last traces of division soften.

Two worlds remain present for a moment longer. One is vast and without form, already receding. The other is immediate and alive, filled with weight, movement, and clarity. Awareness holds them both until the space between them tightens and stills.

The silence deepens. Then the voice of Om arises, resonant and unmistakable, sounding through me with force and authority.

You are a whale, a giant female sperm whale, a divine Lumarian queen.

You are Una.

You carry a witness.

He will remain with you, silent and enduring, as you move through what is, what was, and what may yet be.

And as I dive deeper, letting the currents of clarity guide me, understanding settles without effort. I move as both observer and observed, memory carried alongside instinct rather than replacing it. The weight of the past travels with me, as does the quiet promise of what the ocean may yet teach.

Each stroke and measured flick of my massive tail becomes a living expression of this union, worlds moving together without losing their distinction.

I am Una.

Ishmael is with me.

I am the whale.

Chapter Two

"The Ocean's Embrace"

As this realization settles in my mind, my awareness shifts outward once more. I see the sun clearly and unmistakably. It is shared between both realms, shaped by where I am. Above the surface, it feels thinner, clearer, almost weightless. Below, where movement carries me, the light breaks and drifts, never settling in one place. Breath falls away, becoming something deeper than inhalation; it is harnessed and transformed within me, pouring into my blood and lighting every cell with life.

My vantage is unique as I emerge above the water, looking out across the surface of the ocean in which I live. There is a horizon, and there are clouds, like dollops of white cream against a blue sky. Wonder stirs within me at the familiarity of sight and sound. But there are also humming songs, sharp and unfamiliar. Instinct kicks in and sends me downward. I dive deeper to escape them as they fade into soft echoes, until they disappear entirely. Only in the deep do I feel steady again, my awareness slipping back into the ancient memory of my Lumarian life, shaped long before this moment.

There is a warm presence moving through me, a human awareness learning my body from within. His essence does not speak. It listens as I move through water, feeling pressure and hearing sound. My instincts remain my own, shaped by depth and motion, yet his consciousness awakens inside them, discovering what it means to inhabit a form born of the ocean. The tension between us is not division, but adjustment, a gradual settling into shared sensation. And yet something deeper calls me downward, into the ocean's embrace, where silence gathers and the water begins to soothe every thought as I swim. My skin evokes a slick, seemingly impenetrable layer of protection, like a smooth and seamless shield. The water presses through each striation. I hear only my heartbeat in the stillness of deep water. Its rhythm loosens the tension inside me and softens the edges of thought.

In this calm, clarity does not arrive all at once. Like drops of rain returning to the ocean, it gathers slowly. I feel the ocean not as a place, but as a presence I depend on completely. Like a suckling infant, I need it more than it needs me. Where did it come from? Who put it here? It sustains me as it has sustained all life, those above and below, each living in its own circle within a greater whole. It is gentle in its calm, unpredictable in its shifts, and destructive when agitated. A dual nature reveals itself here, as it does in all living creatures, two legged, four legged, swimming, crawling, and flying.

With this understanding, I let the ocean guide me into its quiet embrace as I dive deeper, feeling the pressure change and fear dissipate. The water cools as I descend, growing denser against my skin. Sound thins to a low, distant hum, stretched and softened by depth. My body adjusts without effort, each movement slower and more deliberate, shaped by the weight around me. I drift from the visions of the world above, released from its presence. In deep water, safety returns as predators thin. There is a softness to the silence here. Sinking below offers a certain knowing.

This is the same world which my ancestors have bathed in for millions of years. There are no debates or quarrels in the deep blue depths in this part of the world, only a wellspring of life-giving waters filled with the songs of Aquarius. I am a seeker of something deeper and more meaningful as I push the boundaries of my body and mind. The pressure is intense, but it provides the setting for serenity and release. Maybe there are answers I'll discover through my psychic dive into the unconscious abyss.

I am where I need to be. The water holds me as pressure ebbs and flows through my body, carrying with it a low, steady music. The rhythm moves in waves, slow and deliberate, a sound felt as much as heard. I drift with each measured pulse. My breath slows. My heartbeat steadies. Darkness gathers gently as I sink deeper, awareness softening into stillness.

Visions return to where they began, and I am slow to wake, remembering the warmth of a quiet place that exists only between layers of sleep, within the absence of awareness. I remain with the moment, tuning into my surroundings, the pressure of the water pressing inward, shaping every cell of my being. I feel a deep connection to this environment and to the unscripted, uncontrolled movements that feel ephemeral and instinctive rather than deliberate. Soon, I will return to the surface for another breath.

A slight fog blurs my thoughts as they drift between two worlds. Why do I feel I was above the surface of this ocean before? Not only within the water, but upon land, where humans dwell. Am I awake or dreaming? This is not the first time I have felt this. I have been here before, among noise and air. I am connected to that life as well, though the thoughts arrive too quickly to settle. Feelings of angst and empathy surface together, flashing past before they can be understood. Where are they coming from? I am awake now, and the peace begins to recede as awareness returns.

My slow and steady ascent brings with it the sights of the place in which I live, filling me with wonder and a quiet affection. Other creatures move through this world, familiar and astonishing. Are our two worlds truly so different? I see life above and below in all its forms. Light and darkness. Hope and fear. Instinct and choice. Life and death. Where am I meant to be? Where do I belong? I surface and draw in the air, taking in the world around me. The noise is gone. I release the thoughts that once clouded my mind and make room for another dive.

Chapter Three

"The Calling of Motherhood"

My journey is short-lived as I sense something upon me. I am not alone. Splashing ripples through the surrounding water. Is there a predator near? A sudden urgency grips me, and I begin to descend. Before long, I realize it is one of my own.

First, there is one whale. Then there are two. Soon it becomes clear there are five whales pursuing me, though I do not yet understand why. Do we turn on our own? Am I in danger? This is not like the visions I have carried of hunters above the surface who chased my ancestors for their flesh. This pursuit feels different. It feels personal.

Understanding arrives with startling clarity. I am female, and my pursuers are male. Yes, this is personal. It is carnal. I am the object of their desire. How has this unfolded so quickly? I continue onward for what feels like an endless stretch of water, until the chase thins and finally slows. I am exhausted, yet no longer afraid. Two males remain. Each vies for my body until only one endures, and the victor impregnates me. It is nature's raw reminder of her dominion.

Mobius, the mighty white whale, emerges from the crucible of survival. His massive form carries the authority of countless generations, shaped by endurance rather than chance. Slowly, he closes the distance between us. I yield, floating near the surface, suspended between the waters above and the depths below, belonging to both. In this liminal space, time loosens its hold. Mobius plants his seed. A moment passes between us, brief and wordless, yet weighted with permanence. Then, with steady grace, he departs.

For a time, I drift without direction. My body feels heavier, yet steadier, as though a new gravity has settled within me. The water holds me differently now. My breath moves slower, deeper, and each pulse carries an unfamiliar resonance, a quiet insistence that does not ask for understanding. Something has taken root, not as thought or intention, but as presence. I do not name it. I carry it within me, settled deep, moving with me through every shift of water and breath.

I return to the pod, changed by what has passed between us.

Understanding rises later, without force. What I once felt as comfort or wonder reveals itself as something older and deliberate. The song that soothed my mind did not remain contained within me. It moved through my body, settled there, then pressed outward, carrying intention. It was a living signal, shaped to travel.

I did not know then that I would first receive it, absorbing its meaning before I could name it, and later carry it forward as part of an ancient rhythm older than memory. It reached beyond my own boundaries, calling to those who knew how to listen. It was the voice of the wild in its most intimate form, a sound marking readiness and passage. A song arriving quietly and precisely, signaling the threshold of motherhood and guardianship, the moment one becomes a vessel not only for life, but for continuity itself.

There is a song within each of us that longs to be sung and shared. Music surrounds us always, though we notice only what we choose, while nature continues along her unwavering course. This song carries something sacred. It is sung for a queen and her princess yet to come. I listen carefully. I heed its message.

Though her arrival still rests in its earliest beginnings, my love has already begun to bloom. She moves through me like a warm summer current, stirring my soul and binding us together in a deep, ethereal way. Ours is a connection that reaches beyond form and time, a light shared between mother and child that can illuminate even the darkest waters. I will honor it. I will trust my instincts to guide her, protect her, and offer her the fullness of a mother's love.

When she enters this world, her name is Kai.

With Kai's arrival, a love unlike anything I have known surges through me, deeper than the farthest trenches, wider than the open sea. Joy rises in waves so powerful they leave me breathless. Braided within it is something new, a vigilance that sharpens every sense. This is not fear born of weakness, but the ancient burden of motherhood, the instinct that has driven females across all species and ages to unimaginable strength.

In my tenderness, there is softness beyond measure. In my protection, there lives a quiet ferocity. I understand without thought or language that I would become unstoppable against anything that threatens her. This knowledge does not frighten me. It clarifies me.

I move through these emotions with awareness, even as my body navigates the water with effortless grace. Each day becomes a shared lesson. I teach Kai how to dive deep and rise gently, how to draw breath at the surface and trust the buoyancy of her growing strength. I guide her first breaches, her body still uncertain as she launches skyward and returns in a cascade of foam and sound that echoes through the pod.

Our bond intensifies with every passing tide.

Kai swims close to me, her movements anticipating mine. We sleep side by side, her small form tucked against my flank, her heartbeat a steady rhythm I carry even as I rest. We share food and play, song and silence. I show her how to listen to the currents, to distant calls, to subtle shifts that signal change. I teach her to hide within floating seaweed while I gather food. When she falters, I slow. When she surges ahead, I follow, watching with pride as her confidence grows.

There is a symbiosis between us that requires no instruction. Communication flows without effort, a shared understanding that makes us feel like one being moving through the sea in two bodies. As Kai's strength increases, we dive to greater depths together, the darkness no longer intimidating but inviting, a place of learning rather than fear.

I have known love before, the affection between playmates, the shared bond of the pod. This is different. The bond between parent and child is elemental and unyielding. It is joy in its purest form, carrying a weight that demands constant presence.

Still, I would not trade it.

I carry my duty gladly, knowing this fierce, radiant connection the great creator entrusted to me is the greatest gift the ocean has ever given.

Time passes, as the ocean allows, without asking permission. Kai grows strong and long, her once soft body now carrying the promise of power, though not yet its full command. She swims beside Una as a young adolescent whale, still learning the balance between instinct and endurance, curiosity and caution.

Then comes the day when caution is no longer enough.

The whale hunters arrive in the waters Una, Kai, and the pod call home. The pod feels it first as a tightening in the currents, a subtle violence carried through sound and vibration long before the boats appear. Una's body reacts before thought can form. She surges forward, calling out in low, urgent tones that ripple through the pod like a warning bell. They are not alone. A threat is closing in.

They flee as one. The ocean erupts with motion. Great tails drive downward, churning water into white chaos as the pod races toward deeper currents. Una stays close to Kai, matching her pace, guiding her with gentle nudges and sharp vocal commands meant to steady her breath and strengthen her resolve.

But Kai struggles.

Her movements falter. Her breaths shorten. Panic threads through her young body as the distance between them and the hunters fails to widen. Una slows instinctively, circling Kai, positioning her massive body between her child and the unseen threat behind them. Every instinct urges her to flee, but love demands something else.

She swims tighter, closer, urging Kai forward with every ounce of will she possesses. The pounding of her heart, the strain in Kai's muscles, the pull of the pod surging ahead, all press against her at once. The ocean seems to hold its breath. In that moment, caught between survival and devotion, Una understands that love does not always outrun danger.

Sometimes, it faces it.

Chapter Four

"Marcus Deep: A Retrospective Glimpse"

Before Marcus Deep became "Captain Marcus," there was a young man with dreams of his own. He planned to express himself through writing, and to expand his horizons beyond the small Newport village where he and past generations had called home. He carried a vulnerability that was eventually taken from him by the basic demands of survival. The shadow of desperation hovered over young Marcus, and the call to duty forced him away from his personal ambitions. Strong and broad shouldered, he became the obvious candidate to bear the weight of his family and village.

Unfair as it may have seemed, the stoic Marcus accepted the challenge and kept his reluctant reservations to himself. A man must provide for his family, sometimes at all costs. It was the creed that justified every harpoon thrown and every tour he sailed on the unforgiving sea. Providing was not just a choice, it was the burden carried by men like him. In his thoughts, strength was not for glory, but for the guardianship of family. The sea teaches this, the blood remembers it, and my ancestors demand it. Provision became duty. Duty became sacrifice. Sacrifice, he told himself, was what made a man. Young Marcus Deep would take this mantra more seriously as time went on, nearly to obsession, especially after he became a father. A new path was forged through the ocean, a whaling boat armed with harpoons. It was not a thirst for blood or profit that beckoned him. It was hunger. Raw, unadulterated hunger.

Often, it was in the early hours of the morning when hunger spoke the loudest. These were moments that invited reflection. The contrast between abundance and need never revealed itself more sharply than in those pre-dawn hours, especially for a man who measured uncertainty through the eyes of his family. To go without as an individual was one thing. The guilt, shame, and insecurity carried far more weight when hunger reached the ones he loved.

There was plenty and then there was none, and it seemed to come upon them like a perfect storm. Today must be the day, he thought, as he sharpened his harpoon and chewed his small ration of stale bread. Packing up his last supplies, he headed out to meet the other two men of the crew, where they would board their small whaleboat in hopes of spearing one. Yes, today must be the day they brought good news to their families and to the small fishing village, where good news had grown scarce. Even a glimpse of hope would be a welcome change.

The short walk to the wharf stirred Marcus to full wakeful gait, and the cold morning air invigorated him. He hoped the long day ahead would prove fruitful. His two mates were already in sight. He thought of their childhood in this same village, where generations of families had been raised. It had been a simple and wonderful place. The smell of the sea lived in their clothes, and fishing ran in their blood. It had been a tough life, one none of them could have imagined. Seen through hindsight, this was not part of their youthful hopes and dreams.

Marcus wanted to be a writer who would one day pen a great novel of adventure and travel, like so many of the books he spent hours reading. His imagination ranged freely through stories of bravery and stoicism. He toyed with poetry and even caught the attention of locals with his writing. His gift was the written word, but fishing chose him out of necessity. It claimed his youth early, driven by the need to help his family put food on the table.

His brother and first mate, Giles, had a natural propensity for numbers and wanted to be an accountant for the local businesses. He was an organized lad who valued planning and order. His contributions would have come through finance, helping to steady the budget and economy of their fishing village.

Thad, the youngest of the three, was the only one who had wanted to be a fisherman, though he imagined it differently. He dreamed of owning his own fleet, of coordinating several boats each day. He hoped to make an impact in the fishing market, providing fresh seafood to small communities along the coast. Thad had even researched the ports he once hoped to serve. Those ambitions had since faded into shadow, overtaken by their present position and its far heavier burden.

The Deep family grew up playing kickball along cobblestone streets and alleyways, their games fueled by laughter and a ramshackle ball stitched from old cloth and bound with fishing twine. They laughed and roughhoused like most young boys, enjoying a simple but memorable childhood in Newport village. The sea seemed more bountiful then, with each family preparing dishes of fish, octopus, and lobster. Neighbors shared in the daily catches. Everyone did their part, and the village thrived. The scent of the ocean was everywhere, and it meant security for their families. Over time, that part of the ocean was worked over by generations of fishing, and the need to venture farther began to press them toward other means of survival.

With the recent sighting of whales offshore, hunting emerged as a viable option. Only a few months earlier, a wounded whale had washed ashore, injured in a violent struggle at sea. The villagers harvested what they could, meat, blubber, even bone. It fed many, and the idea of whale hunting took hold among those brave or desperate enough to consider it. Newport was no Nantucket, yet the sea still whispered of opportunity.

For Marcus and the others, the sight of the whale stirred something older than ambition. It echoed stories passed down through generations of men in his family, accounts spoken without pride or shame, simply as facts of survival. The first impulse was not profit, but tradition, inherited skill, and learned knowledge. Over time, perspectives shifted as they recognized the added value of whale oil for lighting and blubber for soap making, though the most immediate need remained the food provided by the meat itself.

The cold salt air had weathered their skin, and the harsh conditions had hardened their hearts, traits that seemed necessary for whale hunters. The fear of loss cut deeper than any other fear, forging courage in the face of danger. None of these men would have chosen whale hunting, but it had become a necessary means to an end. With steel in their eyes and focus fixed on the task ahead, they boarded the whaleboat one by one.

Each man stowed his modest supplies: harpoons, toggles, knives, homemade gloves, a few pints of ale, dried meat, a half loaf of bread, netting, and rope. Families from the village had pooled what little they could for these young men, who carried not only their own fate, but that of their loved ones as well. Their target would be a smaller whale, as the strength of a larger one would easily overwhelm their narrow craft.

Having prepared their coordinates over the previous week, the whale hunters took their positions, untied the whaleboat from the dock, and paddled out to the open sea. With practiced strokes, they rowed into the widening ocean as the wharf and village they called home faded from sight. Conversation remained light and plentiful, masking the concerns each of them carried. Returning without a catch was not an option.

No one admitted fear. No one spoke of hunger. All three understood what failure meant. Rationing had already begun among many of the village families, their supplies dwindling as the need for food pressed to the forefront of every mind. And with each stroke that carried them farther from home and shore, they drifted just as surely from the personal dreams and futures they had once imagined.

Chapter Five

"The Hunt"

Marcus and his crew moved with quiet certainty, their attention trained on every ripple and shadow around the boat, knowing the waiting could last for hours or end without reward. In recent weeks whale pods had been sighted more often, and with that came a familiar calculation, shaped by distance, depth, and the way bodies moved together on the surface. The calves stayed close to their mothers, surfacing when the larger bodies did, bound to their rhythm. They could not dive as deep or as long. They could not vanish the way the adults could when danger pressed downward.

The men traded rowing for lookout duty with few words, passing a flask between them, tearing at bread and dried meat with salt-stiffened fingers as oars dipped and lifted in a steady rhythm. No one needed instruction. As dawn spread its thin light across the water, heavy coats were shrugged off one by one, and the day opened before them, long, exposed, and patient.

"To the left!" Giles shouted, the sound cracking sharp across the water, urgency flaring through the last trace of ale.

Thad and Marcus leaned harder into their oars, the wood flexing and groaning as brine sprayed cold into their faces. Ahead, the surface broke and settled again. Two adult females moved with unhurried power, their bodies rising and slipping beneath the light, while nearby the calves stayed close, slower in their descent, surfacing longer before sinking again.

"Quiet," Marcus said at once, leaning forward. "Keep it quiet now. Not a sound."

The words barely carried over the slap of water against the hull, but the effect was immediate. Each man froze as warmth drained from their limbs and the last trace of the buzz slipped away, leaving the young sailors hollow and alert. Thad tilted back his flask anyway, trusting the burn to steady him, but the bitterness caught in his throat as his hands betrayed him with a brief tremor.

"Blasted," he muttered under his breath. "Why's it always so bloody early?"

Eyes moved to harpoons and toggles, fingers checking grips and positioning, testing weight and reach. The first light caught the wet grain of the boat and slid across the whales' backs, gray-silver curves breaking the surface before sinking again. Breath was drawn and held, then released slowly, each man settling into the narrow space between movement and restraint, waiting for the signal that would tip them forward.

Marcus's jaw tightened. "Easy now. Steady." The oars pulled back against him, solid and resistant, the water answering each stroke with weight. Somewhere beneath the rhythm, the pull of tide and current asserted itself, a resistance he had learned to read and respect long before he ever commanded a boat. They were close now, close enough that there would be no drifting back. What came next would mark the work they had set themselves to do, whether any of them spoke of it afterward or not.

They were within striking distance before the mother sensed them. Una turned hard, her body cutting across the water as she pressed Kai away from the boat, but the calf answered late, struggling to match the sudden change in direction.

"Onward!" Marcus shouted.

Thad and Giles released their oars with one hand and reached for their spears as the boat surged forward, strokes shortening and quickening all at once.

"Go," Thad said, breathless now.

The distance collapsed. Marcus moved to the bow, spear balanced and ready as the calf surfaced again, too close to the boat, too slow to slip beneath it.

"Steady," Giles said, barely above the water.

Una surged back, striking the surface as she tried to draw the hunters after her. For a moment the water churned with crossing paths and broken lines, bodies cutting and recutting the same space, until the distance between hunter and calf collapsed completely and there was no room left for correction.

The first spear struck Kai low along her side, the impact jolting her body sideways as the surface broke hard around her. Before she could turn, two more spears followed, lines snapping taut as they found their hold.

The sea clouded almost at once. Blood spread and thinned as the wounded calf pulled the boat through the water, the drag of the lines and the weight against her body shortening her strength until the motion failed and she went still. The surface settled into a slow, uneven roll that did not belong to the tide.

Una reached her too late. She circled once, then again, pressing close as the calf was drawn away from her, the space between them widening despite her effort. The sound she made did not rise or carry. It tore, something pulled loose and left open in the water.

The mates did not celebrate. The boat had to be steadied, turned, kept from drifting sideways as they set their course back toward shore. Marcus called for the weight to be shifted. Thad answered and moved without looking at him. Giles braced himself at the gunwale and said the line was holding.

Minutes passed that way as the boat settled into its return course. The calf's body rode alongside the hull, bumping softly as the water shifted. None of them acknowledged it. Their attention stayed divided between rope, oar, and horizon, eyes lifting often to scan the surface for any sign of movement that did not belong to them. Blood carried. They knew what followed it. Each man chose his focus and kept it there, watching for fins, for shadows, for anything drawn in by the work they were already committed to finishing.

In the distance, the mother lingered behind them, rising once before sinking back into the water. She did not close the distance. She did not turn to follow. With each stroke, the space between them widened, the weight alongside the hull carrying the boat steadily out of her reach. Marcus looked once, then turned away. He cleared his throat and raised his voice. "Row swift, but steady."

The hours stretched ahead of them. Positions were kept. Balance was watched. Eyes stayed moving across the water for any sign of fins or shadow that might close in on what they carried. When the tension finally eased, it did so unevenly. Giles let out a breath he had not realized he was holding. Thad passed the flask without comment. The burn did little, but the boat was moving, the weight secure alongside them, and the worst of the uncertainty had fallen away.

The relief was brief and contained.

The air was already turning toward winter. The work they had done would matter before long.

Una drifted without direction, her body moving long after purpose had left it. Sensation dulled, then thinned, as if the water itself had gone quiet around her. She searched the space where Kai had been, again and again, turning through the same darkening circle. There was no answering presence. Only the water, holding the distance where her calf had been.

Chapter Six

"The Mother and The Abyss"

Grief did not arrive as a thought.
It came as weight.

A heaviness inside the ribs, as if the ocean itself had climbed into her chest and refused to leave. Her fins trembled; her great muscles felt suddenly useless, like a ship's sails hanging in windless air. Sound dulled around her. Even the call of the pod seemed distant and distorted, as though she were hearing them from the bottom of the deepest trench. The mere image seemed unfathomable.

Within her, Ishmael felt the change as a tightening and a drag, observing the subtle disruption of a rhythm that had always been sure. Something essential had shifted in the relationship between body and water. The world no longer moved with her. Resistance met her motion, gently at first, then with growing insistence.

Although her baby's spirit would forever live in her heart, and pervade her very existence, this served no consolation to the mother whale. Physical presence and warmth had shaped their bond. Their connection had been built through closeness, touch, and shared movement, through the constant assurance of one body alongside another. No memory could replace that.

She remembered the way Kai had learned to curve her small body through the surge, surprised by her own grace. She remembered the wobbling first dives, the playful nudges, the joy whales share through motion rather than sound. That life had been simple. It had been whole. It had been theirs.

Guilt made it impossible for Una to hold the memory of what she had witnessed without distortion. A part of her knew the hunters had cast the harpoon. Another part whispered more dangerous thoughts.

I should have been faster.

I should have seen it coming.

I should have kept her closer.

The cruelest voice did not belong to the men. It belonged to herself.

The images did not simply replay. They rewrote themselves. She saw the harpoon flying again and again, but each time it was her hesitation that guided its path. Grief is cruel in this way as it turns tragedy into accusation. The ocean around her held no judgment. The men in the whaleboat did not know her name. Yet the voice inside Una rose like a storm, persistent and unyielding.

I failed her.

I failed my own heart.

She was broken in every possible way. Out of anger and desperation, Una accelerated without warning, driving herself forward with reckless abandon, away from her mother, Astra, and the pod that had borne witness to Kai's murder. Ishmael felt the acceleration as rupture. Grief translated itself into force, into speed that bordered on violence, as though motion itself might outrun what remained behind.

Astra followed as best she could, but she was helpless all the same. She had lived long enough to witness the devastation of whales being killed more times than she wished to remember. This loss struck differently. With the death of her grandchild, Astra felt a part of herself torn away as well.

Astra did not weep the way humans do. Her grief moved through her in other ways, traveling through muscle and current, carried in the low songs that trembled out of her body and into the sea. She had known loss before. She had watched ships appear on horizons that should have held only light. She had seen calves taken, mates fall silent, and the seas grow thinner of life with each passing season.

But this was different.

This was her daughter's child.

Grief, when it reaches the level of lineage, becomes something more than pain. It becomes an inheritance. Astra felt it pulsing through her blood, through Una's blood, through whatever deep mystery would come after their existence.

With each ripple of the ocean lived the layered trauma Astra carried, pain for her daughter entwined with grief for her granddaughter. Astra spoke inwardly, to the vastness, to the ancestors she could no longer see but still felt in the water all around her body:

Take care of her.

Take care of both of them.

I cannot hold this alone.

She had taught Una to listen for the songs beneath the surface of things, the currents that remembered everything. Now those same currents carried a new note, low and aching, threading through the water like a wound. Astra understood that this grief would not dissolve with time. It would change shape, as grief always does, and continue living within those who survived. She held no illusion that nature was fair. She had lived too long for that. But until now, she had believed that love alone was enough to protect the young. That belief broke apart, and she felt the fragments settle deep into her bones.

The grief was generational, coursing through the currents like an unbroken chain. The gruesome vision she had witnessed would remain with her for all her days, pressing against her soul with relentless fervor. In a single merciless sweep, the hunters had taken three lives, and though one now rested in peace, the other two would carry the echoes of human cruelty forward, as all life does, through the eternal passage of time. This had been the way of the world since humans first set foot upon the Earth, and yet the sting of it felt unbearably immediate.

Without Kai, there was no beauty or joy left in her life. Nothing aligned the way it used to. Once at home in two realms, beneath the water and above its surface, Una now felt anchored to neither. What had once carried her without question now offered no place to rest. The surface, bright with scattered sunlight, held no invitation. The deep, once steady with darkness and familiar silence, no longer sheltered her.

Now both realms felt foreign, as though she were a guest in a body she no longer wished to inhabit.

Una's pain was not physical. Sensation had left her body entirely. She cried out for her baby as her speed slowed and her body tipped downward, diving toward the deep abyss. Delirium crept in alongside her grief as she gradually returned to the surface and drew in another breath. In her exhaustion, there was nowhere left to turn but toward the shore, where she would remain through the night. Una surrendered herself to the tide's slow pull and release one final time.

The cold air stung against her skin as rain fell the next morning. She had once loved the rain. It brought rhythm and a quiet sense of renewal. She and Kai had watched droplets scatter across the surface of the sea, their world alive with movement and sound. This time, the rain returned stripped of comfort, settling over her as cold, isolation, and the unmistakable absence of what had been.

Once, she had lifted her head toward the storm simply to feel the rain strike her skin, delighting in the way each drop scattered across her body. She laughed in the only way whales can, through motion rather than sound, through spirals carved into the water, through joy that radiated outward and stirred the sea itself. Her movements had been light then, buoyed by a world that still felt intact, still capable of surprise and abundance.

Now the rain pressed against her with weight and consequence, each drop landing as if it carried the memory of what had been lost. It drove her deeper into the certainty that the world she had known no longer existed in the way it once had. The ocean moved around her as it always had, but she felt estranged within it, as though something essential had slipped beyond reach.

Without Kai, the idea of renewal unraveled. Beauty and continuity no longer formed a path forward. The thought of continuing in a world that did not include her daughter felt hollow and unsustainable, stripped of meaning. While the village would be sustained by Kai's body and life would move forward through her sacrifice, Una would take her final breath at the edge of the earth. She would lie upon the sand, her massive form still, listening as the sound of the waves gradually thinned and faded from her awareness. Despair carried her past any thought of return. That others would live because of her child's body offered no consolation. Una would choose to follow Kai into the darkness beyond death. Her will was exhausted. Her heart could not endure a future that did not include the one it had formed itself around.

Beneath the crushing weight of her grief, another awareness began to surface. It offered no relief and no promise of comfort, only a widening sensation, as though the boundary between worlds were loosening. As the shoreline cradled her failing body, Una felt a vast presence opening around her. It was neither hostile nor consuming. It waited. The darkness did not advance. It received her. Her final thoughts drifted between fragments of joy and loss as her mind released memories of herself and her daughter, each one briefly held before dissolving into stillness.

Astra sang.

The song rose from a depth older than language, carried by whales since the beginning of their remembering. It moved through the water as resonance, binding what had lived to what endured beyond form. The current carried it across great distance and into the sand where Una lay dying. Whether Una perceived it no longer mattered.

Songs like this are not taken in through hearing alone.

They are carried within the being itself.

Somewhere beyond body and water, beyond the names that had once defined her, Astra sensed that the story had not reached its end. Grief was carving a passage through their lineage, shaping what would come after. One day, someone would walk that passage and carry forward what had been lost, shaping it into something that could endure.

Within that widening stillness, Ishmael became aware of himself again. He did not enter the moment. He had been there all along, carried within the unfolding, bound to it without voice or body of his own. He sensed the shift as recognition, as separation. Something had been broken open, not to end, but to change. What was passing through Una did not stop with her. It moved onward, toward a future form.

As Una's final breath left her body, the ocean continued its rhythm. In the darkness that received her, something ancient swelled and became attentive. The current altered its course through intention alone, and what had been broken did not vanish. It gathered and was held.

Beyond both depth and surface, a presence older than storms became aware.

The abyss listened.

And it prepared its reply.

Chapter Seven

"The Decree of Om"

The clouds dissipate as the rainfall slowed to a trickle. The splash of the tidewater at the shore slapped against the massive, stiff body that Una once inhabited. The flesh belongs to her no more, for the journey of a soul that passes through lifetimes may change vessels, while faint links remain connected. What once provided a comfortable home to her being, will serve as sustenance for nature's other creatures. Once picked over by animals and man alike, Una's former body will decompose and its remains will return to the Earth, both in water and land where she once felt connected.

The whale body is gone! Her spirit is transitioning to a place where her thoughts, fears, hopes, emotions, and dreams will no longer weigh heavily upon her being. What once belonged to Una and her spirit companion, Ishmael, now belongs to the earth, wind, sea, and sun. Ishmael's watchful presence begins to fade as Una's spirit is surrounded by quiet darkness.

Om's words are powerful and succinct and they reverberate through Una like a thousand tiny pin pricks against the soul.

"I am sending you back!"

These words played over in Una's mind, with each echoing utterance, and there was a brief pause while she processed the message from Om.

"You will be born into the whale hunter family who took Kai from you."

Una wanted to scream, although she knew it would be of no help to her plea.

"Why would you have me be born into a house of whale hunters?" Una pleaded with Om, her sorrow echoing through the unseen currents of darkness. "They took my child from me, the deepest love my life ever knew."

Om's voice was strong but compassionate as he continued, "It was not meant for you to take your own life. You will return and you will learn to value and love life in all forms and varieties." The words were resolute and unwavering. Una pleaded, "But they killed my baby! What about Kai's life, was it all in vain?" Una continued, "Her grace, beauty, and innocence were taken by the very beings you are making me become. Anything but a whale hunter! How about a bug, a flower, a tree? Something that doesn't harm another, as I'm tired of being witness to pain and suffering."

As Una's words to Om humbly came to an end, she hoped her appeal would change the outcome. It did not take but a few moments of silence before she slowly surrendered, recognizing that her argument was futile.

"It was my will that Kai's body was taken; her flesh kept the hunters' families alive through a harsh winter. Your journey and her life shall not be in vain, as you gain another worldly perspective, you will begin to understand the circle of life. This is not a punishment, but an opportunity for you to grow and appreciate life." Om exclaimed.

In that moment, Una's spirit was moved upon like a sail in the wind.

Chapter Eight

"Born into the Deep"

The room was heavy with anticipation. Elizabeth's breath came in short, measured bursts as the waves of labor carried her closer to the moment she had long awaited. Marcus, tense and alert, held her hand, his knuckles white, his mind split between the immediacy of the birth and the endless rhythm of the sea he had always known. The midwife murmured instructions, but Elizabeth hardly heard them, her focus elsewhere, on the life stirring within her.

And then, with a final cry that seemed to echo in the quiet of the room, Homer entered the world.

Elizabeth's arms wrapped around him instinctively. A shiver passed through her, subtle and unexplainable, as if something larger than her own heart had moved through the infant. Marcus leaned closer, studying the tiny, fragile form, sensing something in the way Homer's fingers flexed, in the weight of his body resting against hers. There was a stillness about him, a quiet presence that both unsettled and awed them. But it was in Homer's eyes that Marcus felt it most clearly. The child's gaze held a depth that did not belong to infancy alone. It was not knowledge in any form he could name, but a presence that seemed to watch him in return. Something in that look carried sorrow and patience, as though grief had already passed through and left understanding behind.

Unseen, Una's essence moved gently into the newborn, meeting no resistance. Guided by Om, it took its place in this human vessel, bringing whispers of the ocean, memories of tides and currents, and a soft echo of grief and longing. This consciousness, once vast and free in the waters of another life, settled subtly into Homer's being, threading through his senses, his instincts, and the quiet spaces of his mind that would one day stir with the faintest déjà vu.

Elizabeth rocked him, feeling a warmth that was both familiar and enigmatic, a sense that this child carried more than the sum of his parents' love. Marcus, still cautious and practical, sensed it too, although not in words, but in a shift in the air, the room, and the world. Something had arrived with Homer that neither lineage nor duty could fully account for. A presence older than time had entered, and with it, the first threads of a journey that would weave together human life, the ocean's mysteries, and the long path toward redemption and forgiveness in human form.

In that quiet, trembling moment, life and destiny converged. Homer's cries softened into a calm, rhythmic breath. It was the same breath that once surged through Una beneath the waves. The child slept, yet already he was listening, feeling, absorbing. Marcus and Elizabeth, unaware of the extraordinary transformation taking place, held him close, guardians to a spirit whose path would chart both the beauty and the pain of existence. As the first light of morning filtered through the window, the cycle continued: life, death, rebirth, and the silent promise of redemption carried in the gentle curl of a newborn's hand.

In the quiet hours after Homer's birth, the village beyond the windows was already stirring. Salt tang and seaweed drifted in on the morning breeze, carrying the faint cries of gulls and the steady slap of tidewater against the shore. Marcus, exhausted yet vigilant, gently placed Homer into Elizabeth's arms again, feeling the weight of responsibility settle like a stone in his chest. For him, this was not merely a child; it was a continuation of a lineage forged by the sea, by struggle, and by survival.

Elizabeth, pale but radiant, traced the curve of Homer's cheek with a trembling finger, her thoughts swimming between relief, awe, and something indefinable. She sensed a depth in her son, a presence that seemed to listen even in slumber. She whispered his name softly, as if naming him could somehow anchor the vast mystery she felt coiling within the infant. And perhaps it did. Somewhere beneath the surface, a spirit not entirely of this world had taken residence, carrying with it echoes of waves, currents, and a life lived in the rhythm of the ocean.

Outside, the village stirred to its familiar rhythm. Nets were drawn taut and repaired, boats were nudged into readiness, oars creaked against their locks, and water lapped steadily against weathered hulls. The sounds carried the assurance of routine, the comfort of work begun as it always had. Inside the modest home, however, time seemed to loosen its grip, stretching into something quieter and more inward.

Marcus sat with his thoughts drifting backward through the years. The scent of tar and rope returned to him, sharp and grounding. He could almost taste the salt that had once coated his tongue after long days at sea, feel the deep ache in his arms and shoulders earned through labor and endurance. His mind settled on the day he harpooned his first whale, a memory layered with exhilaration and fear, pride tangled with the sudden recognition of consequence. That moment had carried him forward into manhood, followed closely by grief that cut just as deeply. The loss of baby Kai had left an imprint that never fully faded, along with the heavy knowledge that life and death could hinge on a single decision. That understanding had shaped him as surely as the tides shaped the shoreline he had grown up beside.

His gaze dropped to Homer, so small and still in his arms, the rise and fall of the child's breath steady and deliberate, as though guided by an ancient patience. A tight sensation gathered in Marcus's chest, something close to hope, edged with apprehension. He could not yet see the full measure of the boy's spirit or the paths that would one day open before him. He did not know how far those currents would carry him or what trials they would demand.

Even so, something within Marcus settled into quiet certainty. This child was not only a continuation of blood and name, but a calling. He felt it as responsibility, as devotion, and as a challenge that would require more of him than strength alone. In that moment, he understood that Homer was a gift entrusted to him, one that would ask him to grow in ways he had never anticipated.

As the sunlight grew stronger, brushing gold across the village, the first whispers of the life Homer would inherit began to take shape in the minds of his parents. The sea would be both cradle and classroom, the village both sanctuary and proving ground. Marcus's fatherly authority, tempered by the memory of past loss, would cast a long shadow over Homer's childhood. Elizabeth's love and gentle guidance would serve as ballast, holding him steady when the weight of inheritance pressed down too heavily.

And so the cycle carried on, shaped by inheritance and choice, by memory and consequence. Within the newborn, Una's essence stirred softly, not as a presence to be named, but as a quiet intelligence learning the cadence of this new existence. The rhythm of breath, the warmth of human touch, the mingled scents of salt air and hearth smoke, and the distant sounds of the village beginning its day all entered him gently, settling into places deeper than thought.

The earliest lessons were already taking root, lessons of endurance learned through steady care, of empathy absorbed through closeness and need, and of legacy carried not as burden alone, but as continuity. These were not teachings spoken aloud, but impressions formed through living, through being held, through belonging. They wove themselves slowly into the fabric of the boy's becoming, shaping him in ways unseen and unmeasured.

Marcus would change in time, tempered by responsibility and softened by love. The village too would shift and grow, weathered by seasons and sustained by its shared labor. And Homer would grow within that world, carried forward by forces older than memory and nearer than breath. For now, however, the morning belonged to something smaller and more intimate. It belonged to a single inhalation, a single heartbeat pressed against another, a promise formed not in words but in presence. Life would continue in its turning, carrying with it remembrance and renewal, and the child resting in Marcus's arms would one day bear both the visible weight of his lineage and the quieter echoes of a spirit that had once moved freely through the boundless depths of the sea.

The village where Homer would grow up was the same one that had nurtured his father, Captain Marcus, and generations of the Deep family before him. Time had changed both the village and Marcus, yet one constant remained: a reliance on the sea for sustenance and livelihood. Marcus was no longer the boy who had captained a small vessel and harpooned his first whale. That day, he and his crew killed the adolescent whale known as Kai, which was a necessary act, part of the unyielding rhythm of survival that sustained the families of the village through the harsh winter. Through years of experience, Marcus had honed his craft into a disciplined trade, shaped by precision, efficiency, and an unwavering focus on the work at hand.

People now called him Captain Marcus, a whaler in every sense of the word. He governed both ship and household with precision and discipline, his authority forged through years of hard labor, loss, and survival at sea. Order mattered to him. Structure mattered. He believed these were the tools that kept men alive and families intact, and he enforced them with a steadiness that left little room for softness.

To those around him, Marcus carried a formidable presence, one shaped by experience and responsibility, unmistakable and often intimidating. In time, Homer would come to feel the gravity of that presence in his own life. It would loom large in his upbringing, guiding him through expectation and restraint, shaping him as surely as the sea shapes the shoreline, not through gentleness, but through constant and undeniable force.

Although the seaside village had slowly progressed in its own way, Homer's childhood shared the rhythms and routines of generations past. The ocean was their backyard, a boundless playground and a vital provider of food, work, and recreation. From a young age, Homer and his childhood playmates learned to navigate boats, dive into the surf, and cast nets for fish, their small hands growing accustomed to the pull of rope and oar. The village thrived on close-knit connections, where neighbors knew one another, children played freely, families worked together, and Sundays were marked by church services and shared meals. It was a life framed by discipline, community, and the steady, unspoken pulse of the sea.

Homer, however, would experience it with a subtle advantage, the legacy of Captain Marcus already pressing quietly around him. While the Deep family was by no means wealthy, Marcus's tireless work ethic and dedication to provision had spared his household the hardships that had defined previous generations. Hunger, want, and uncertainty were foreign to Homer's early years. He grew up in a time when the labor of his ancestors had become his inheritance, and the fruits of their perseverance were his to enjoy. Life felt balanced between the demands of tradition and the small freedoms of a boyhood by the sea.

Chapter Nine

"Weight of the Harpoon"

By the time Homer was seven, it was unmistakable that his father's will shaped the household. Marcus ruled with a quiet, unyielding authority, honed from years of mastery at sea and inherited from generations of sailors, merchants, and seafarers stretching back to his ancestors. Homer quickly learned that following in his father's footsteps in the family tradition of whale hunting was not a choice. Whale hunting had long been more than survival; it was a craft, a legacy that provided oil, soap, and other goods vital to the village economy. The death of Kai had been one of many that sharpened Marcus's skill and reinforced a relentless drive for efficiency, each kill measured not in sentiment but in results and sustenance for the family.

Like most young boys, Homer looked up to his father as a heroic figure and wanted to spend as much time with him as possible. Marcus, being a stern and strong man, already carried himself with an air of authority and power, so it wasn't much of a stretch for Homer and others to see him in that light. Searching for whales and being out on a boat in the ocean with his father was the only part of whale hunting that Homer enjoyed. Secretly, he hoped they would not find any whales every time they went out. Homer just wanted to spend time with Marcus and his uncles.

Even at this young age, however, Homer sensed a shadow beneath his father's competence. Una's spirit quietly noted these subtleties while observing his unflinching drive, the intensity, the unquestioned command that would soon clash with Homer's emerging conscience and the voice of the whale within him. Yet Homer could not foresee how quickly that shadow would grow, how sharply it would cut into his own understanding of life and death.

The moment arrived sooner than Homer expected.

One gray morning, with mist clinging to the waves, Marcus announced it was time for Homer's first "rite of passage": a full whale hunt. Homer's heart raced with a mixture of fear and excitement. In Marcus's eyes, this was a defining moment, a boy becoming a man. Homer's small hands gripped the rail of the boat as the village receded behind them, leaving only open sea and the anticipation of what was to come. He felt the thrill of adventure, the pride of being chosen to accompany his father, and a deep desire to prove himself. He did his best to keep any unease hidden.

Hours passed in tense silence as Marcus and his crew scanned the water. Homer tried to match his father's calm, but a knot of unease grew in his stomach with each rolling wave. And then they saw it, the ocean misting into the air as a massive shadow moving beneath the surface breached for air. Marcus barked orders, and Homer's pulse quickened.

"There she is," Marcus said, voice steady. "Stay close, Homer. Watch and learn. This is what it means to be a Deep man."

Homer swallowed hard, nodding, but the shadow beneath the waves made his chest tighten.

The whale surfaced, and the boat surged forward. The crew

readied harpoons. Homer's gaze caught the whale's eye, which seemed intelligent, wide, alive. A jolt of fear shot through him.

"Father, can't we let it pass?" Homer whispered, his voice trembling.

Marcus's eyes narrowed. "You're not a man yet, Homer. You learn by doing. We do what is necessary. Do you understand?"

Homer's stomach churned. "But it's… it's alive. It just needs to breathe."

Marcus gritted his teeth. "It's a whale. And we need it. Stay out of my way."

Homer's heart pounded so violently he could feel it beating against his coat. Without thinking, he lunged forward, grabbing the shaft of the harpoon with both hands. "No. Stop. Please, don't."

Marcus froze, startled by the boy's defiance. "God damn it, Homer. Let go. You don't know what you're doing."

"I can't. I… I can't," Homer yelled, tears streaking down his face as the whale's cry echoed across the waves.

Marcus sighed, muscles tense, and finally pried the harpoon from Homer's hands. "You'll learn, boy. One day you'll understand why this is done. But not today." Marcus cast the harpoon, and Homer watched in horror as it flew toward the whale.

Homer stepped back, trembling, his chest heaving. "I… I don't think I ever will." He could feel the thrashing body beneath them, the spray of blood in the air as the whale's lungs filled with it, and his soul ached in ways he had never known. The boat moved on, the whale's massive, lifeless body floating alongside, bobbing with the waves as it trailed behind them. Homer sat frozen, eyes wide and unblinking, feeling the pulsing of the whale's last moments in his own chest. The cries of the whale became an echo in his chest, a heartbeat that was no longer his own.

Marcus worked with precision, each movement practiced and efficient, each decision aimed toward outcome and completion. To him, the hunt was a task that demanded focus and control, nothing more and nothing less. But to Homer, standing on the deck and watching it unfold, the scene felt unbearable. What his father treated as labor registered in his own body as violence, a taking that echoed far beyond the moment itself.

He wanted to turn away. He wanted to run, to shout, to break the stillness with protest. Yet his feet remained fixed to the deck, held there by a sense of obligation he barely understood, a pull born of family loyalty and expectation. His stomach churned as the reality of the act settled into him. His hands trembled at his sides, and beneath the shock and nausea, something darker began to rise. Anger took hold, sharp and insistent, not only toward the act itself but toward the man he loved and admired, the man who could stand so calm and unwavering while a life was ended with such practiced certainty.

What unsettled Homer most was not the killing alone, but the absence of acknowledgment. He felt an ache for something unspoken, a moment of pause, a gesture of recognition for the life that had been taken. In his heart, the ocean was not merely a resource but a living presence, and its creatures deserved respect beyond efficiency. He believed that taking a life demanded reverence, an understanding that such acts carried consequence and meaning. To him, a true hunter honored what was taken, recognizing that survival came with responsibility, humility, and a code shaped by respect rather than profit.

That night, back in the quiet of their home, Homer lay awake, replaying the scene in his mind. The image of the whale's dying eye haunted him. He clenched his fists, whispered protests to the dark, and allowed himself to feel the weight of grief and fury for the first time. He could not yet articulate it, but a seed of rebellion had been planted, along with a simmering awareness that the world he was being inducted into was not entirely the one he wanted to inhabit.

The sounds of the village carried in from outside: the creak of boats shifting at the dock, the rhythmic thud of tools, the distant voices of fishermen already at work harvesting the whale for her flesh, her oil, and whatever else the community required. None of it brought him comfort. Instead, the noise pressed in on him, a reminder of the life that waited for him, a life shaped by routines and expectations that left little room for hesitation or reflection.

Each sound seemed to reinforce the same lesson he had been taught without words. This was a world built on efficiency, on inherited practice, on doing what had always been done because survival demanded it. The whale's body, now reduced to resource and yield, floated in the aftermath of that certainty. Homer felt something tighten inside him as he listened. The work continued as it always had, purposeful and unsentimental, but it stirred a growing unease he could not yet name.

He sensed a quiet conflict taking root within him, a pull toward something different. Even as he understood the necessity of labor and tradition, he felt an instinctive need to acknowledge the life that had been taken, to recognize it as more than material or outcome. That instinct stood at odds with the creed he was expected to inherit, and the tension it created settled deep in his chest. Without speaking it aloud, Homer knew that his way of seeing the ocean and its creatures would never fully align with the one that ruled the village around him.

Chapter Ten

"An Unlikely Kinship"

As Homer wrestled with the weight of that day's hunt in the years that followed, he began to wander along the cliffs at the edge of the village, seeking the ocean's whisper to calm the storm in his chest. It was here, among the salt-scented wind and jagged rocks, that he first saw her: Noko. She was crouched near a tide pool, her fingers tracing the shapes of crabs and shells with gentle reverence, her dark hair falling in loose waves across her shoulders. She belonged to the local Native community, whose roots stretched back through generations across the forests, rivers, and shores surrounding the village. Her presence carried the quiet authority of someone intimately connected to the land and sea.

At first, Homer hesitated. He had never seen anyone move with such care, with such ease among the creatures of the tide. Curiosity overcame his shyness, and he stepped closer.

"What are you doing?" he asked, voice barely above the sound of the waves.

"I'm seeing who belongs here," Noko replied without looking up. "The crabs, the fish, even the shells, they all have a place. We have to respect that."

Homer nodded, though he did not yet grasp the depth of her words. Something in the way she spoke, in the way she observed the world, struck a chord deep in his chest. For the first time since the hunt, he felt a sense of connection that had nothing to do with his father, the whaleboat, or the blood-stained rituals of the village. It came instead from someone who seemed to see life without cruelty or detachment.

From that day forward, they found one another along the edges of the cliffs, the woods, and beside quiet streams. Noko taught him the ways of her people: the importance of balance, of taking only what was needed, of honoring the lives that sustained them. In turn, Homer shared with her the glimpses of sorrow and anger that churned in his heart, the residue of a world that demanded he take life to survive. In their secret meetings, under the shadow of trees or beneath the endless stars, a quiet companionship blossomed. It grew without declaration, rooted in trust, friendship, and a shared reverence for the ocean and the life it held.

At times, something deeper stirred in Homer. A feeling would come to him sporadically and stoke a memory from another time. He could hear the cries of the whales in his dreams and feel a pulsing through his soul like a second heartbeat. He shared these thoughts and emotions with nobody, for fear of hurting his father's feelings and possibly from being ostracized. The only person he felt able to speak of such things with was Noko.

She became more than a friend. To Homer, Noko was a guide, a keeper of the balance that Homer's father seemed blind to, a mirror of the whale's own spirit that still whispered through him. And while he could not yet defy his father, the seed had been planted. Homer understood, in some small instinctive way, that there was a life worth protecting, and a way of being in the world that honored both the ocean and the creatures that called it home.

As they matured over the following years, Homer and Noko would quietly continue to cross paths without ceremony. This would happen sometimes along the shoreline where Homer cast a line into the water, other times at the edge of the fields where the land met the sea. What began as shared glances and wordless understanding slowly formed into a friendship. Out of caution and fear of judgment, they kept their meetings discreet, aware that their connection bridged two worlds not meant, in the eyes of others, to intertwine.

Though they came from different traditions, they were drawn together by a shared reverence for the earth and its living rhythms. With Noko, Homer felt less alone in his unease, less strange in the questions that haunted him. Still, he struggled to make sense of the quiet pull he felt toward her and toward the natural world she understood so intuitively. He often dismissed these feelings as lingering curiosities from childhood or passing fascinations born of youth while remaining uncertain of who he was becoming, and what future awaited him. He did know one thing for certain. It hurt him deeply to see whales being killed. Although he was empathetic to the needs of those who hunted for survival, he could not reconcile himself to the idea of taking an innocent and beautiful life for the sake of profit.

As they grew older, Homer and Noko would sit under the stars at night talking about philosophy and the universe. Noko had an innate connection to nature and would share some of the Native traditions such as respecting the earth and taking from it only what is necessary, like flowers and herbs for medicine, an occasional animal from the land, or fish from the waters for food. Homer would take long walks alone at night as a teenager in hopes of running into Noko, and they began a signaling system leaving messages and symbols like the sun or moon in the sand, which would indicate a meet up at either morning or evening the next day. They did not always respond to the messages because of other constraints, but when they did, it brought a smile to each of their faces and a quiet sense of satisfaction. What began as friendship grew gently and without force, an innocent bond taking root, and one that would shape them both in ways neither yet understood.

On a particularly poignant night, long after they parted, Homer wandered the cliffs above the sea, the tide breathing steadily below him. The moon traced a pale path across the water, and for the first time he sensed that the ocean was not merely vast, but attentively listening, as if to the quiet tides of his heart. The veil between what was seen and what was sensed had begun to soften. A strange calm settled over him, threaded with an unease that had no clear shape, as though something within him had been stirred and left unfinished. When he finally lay down to sleep, the rhythm of the waves followed him into darkness, and with it came the faint impression that he was no longer alone in his thoughts. Whatever had been set in motion that night did not end there. It moved with him, quietly, toward a reckoning yet to come.

Chapter Eleven

"Una Remembers Through Homer"

The rolling sound of thunder came first. Not as words or a voice as Homer would understand it, but as a low bass vibration, vast, and unbroken as it rolled through him like the tide beneath a ship's hull. The presence of Om was with Homer. It echoed without direction, without edge, filling the dark interior of his mind until there was no distance between sound and being. Suddenly, from within that resonance, an unknown name was spoken with reverence.

Una.

Homer felt himself falling inward, drawn through layers of memory that were not his own. The boundaries of his body softened. His breath slowed. And then the water closed around him. He was moving through the deep.

Not as a boy, not as a man, but as something immense and deliberate, a body shaped by centuries of currents and migrations. He felt the power of a great tail driving the body forward, the glide of flesh through cold velvet silence. Sound traveled differently here, not as noise, but as knowing. Songs braided the water, ancient and intimate, carrying stories older than land.

Homer understood then: this was Una's life he was witness to.

He saw her as she had been, a large sperm whale, luminous, and alive. He recognized her body instinctively, the curve of her back, the markings along her flank, the way she surfaced for air. Recognition struck him with grief. He had seen bodies like hers hauled and butchered. He had smelled their blood. He had stood on decks slick with their oil.

The dream shifted.

Joy swelled within his bosom as he witnessed silhouettes playfully spiraling through sunlit water, the nearness of other whales, the comfort of the pod. Then he felt the presence of youth. It was Kai, though at that moment he was unaware of her meaning or significance.

Clarity settled as the calf's presence pulsed with brightness, with clumsy wonder and unrestrained trust. Homer felt the fierce tenderness of motherhood rise in him, protective and absolute. He witnessed Una swim close, guiding, teaching, sheltering.

And then, the sound.

Metal striking flesh.

The water erupted with pain.

Homer felt Una's anguish tear through him as Kai thrashed, her cries splintering the ocean's song. Blood clouded the water, turning light into horror. The grief felt unbearable not only for the loss of her child, but the incomprehension of it. The senselessness. The betrayal of nature's balance.

Una's sorrow hardened into something resolute and final.

Homer felt the moment she chose not to continue.

Her resolve did not emerge from weakness, but from an emotional rupture in a world that no longer made sense. Her body sank. Her song ceased. And yet, she did not disappear.

The darkness gave way to stillness, and in that stillness, Una became something else. No longer bound to flesh, she watched. She followed. Homer saw her dark grey-blue eye focused on his soul and he sensed she did not view him as an enemy, but as a mirror. He felt her resistance soften into curiosity. Her grief into witness.

The voice of Om returned with gentle guidance:

Through you, Una will see what she could not understand.

Through you, she will learn forgiveness without forgetting.

Through you, the wound between hunter and hunted can be healed.

A moment of silence passed as the words settled in Homer's center. Una's essence moved into him deeper for what felt like a close companionship rather than possession.

Remember, the vibration seemed to whisper.

And let remembering change you.

Homer woke with a sharp breath, his heart pounding, his body damp with sweat. Dawn filtered faintly through the room, the world intact but altered. He lay still, afraid that movement would fracture whatever had just passed through him. It felt nascent and unfinished. The questions pressed in immediately.

Why me?

Why now?

Why her?

He found Noko later that day near the cliffs, where the wind carried the smell of salt and kelp. He spoke quickly at first, words stumbling over themselves as he tried to give shape to what he had seen. Then he slowed. He told her everything, describing the sound, the name, the whale, the calf, and the grief that was not his yet lived in him.

Noko did not interrupt but listened intently. When he finished, she was quiet for a long moment, her gaze fixed on the horizon.

"This does not surprise me," she said finally.

Homer turned to her. "It doesn't?"

She shook her head gently. "Some spirits do not leave when their bodies do. They wait. They listen. And sometimes, they choose someone who can carry their remembering."

She looked at him then, really looked at him with a strong focused eye.

"In my people's teachings," she continued, "The whale is a keeper of the ocean's voice. They carry the songs of the water spirit. When balance is broken, those songs find new voices."

Homer swallowed. "So what does it mean?"

Noko placed her hand over his, steady and warm. "It means you are not only who you were born as. You are becoming a dancing warrior to the whales and their songs. And you have been chosen to see through more than one set of eyes."

The ocean moved below them, endless and patient.

Noko's voice softened, but weight remained beneath it.

"My people believe that when something is taken without honor, it does not leave quietly," she said. "Its spirit lingers. Not in anger at first, but in confusion. In waiting."

Homer frowned. "Waiting for what?"

"For balance," she replied. "For acknowledgment. For someone willing to listen."

She gestured toward the sea. "Whales are not just animals to us. They are carriers of memory. They remember who takes from them, and how. When they are hunted with reverence, their spirits return to the ocean's song. But when they are taken without gratitude, without ceremony, the song breaks."

Homer felt his chest grow warm.

"And when a song breaks," Noko continued, "it echoes through bloodlines."

She looked at him carefully now. "Your family has hunted whales for generations. Yes, they fed their people, but somewhere along the way, the remembering was lost. The ocean noticed. The spirits noticed."

Homer's throat tightened. "So… Una found me because of them?"

Noko nodded her head with an affirming gesture. "Not because of them," she said gently. "Because of you."

She placed her hand over his chest. "You are the one who felt the break. You are the one who could not turn away. Spirits do not seek punishment, they seek restoration. Una did not come to haunt you. She came because you could carry what your father could not." Homer stared out at the water, the dream pressing back into him with new clarity.

"My elders teach that when balance is broken," Noko said, "someone is born into the lineage with the burden, and the gift, of seeing clearly. That person walks between worlds. Between past and future. Between hunter and protector."

She met his eyes. "That is why her memory moves through you. Not to condemn your family, but to heal what was left unfinished."

The ocean shifted below them, a slow, breathing presence.

"You are not bound to repeat what came before," Noko added. "You are bound to remember it. What you do with that remembering… that is your choosing."

Homer closed his eyes.

For the first time, Una's presence did not feel heavy. It felt purposeful.

Chapter Twelve

"The Weight of Choosing"

The shoreline breathed in long, slow tides as dawn touched the horizon with pale fire. The world had not changed, and yet nothing was the same. Homer sat with his elbows on his knees, Noko's words echoing through him like the echo of a distant horn blast in the thickness of fog.

You are not bound to repeat what came before.

You are bound to remember it.

Memory did not leave with waking. It stayed as a soothing presence. Una did not hover above him like a haunting. She settled inside him like a second heartbeat. He could feel her the way one feels the breath without seeing it. Pressure, depth, a vastness sensed through the bones.

Images moved through him unbidden.

The slick shine of whale skin under moonlight.

The calf's uncertain movements beside its mother.

The flash of steel.

The tearing of breath from the body.

But something had changed.

The memory did not crush him.

It asked something of him.

He did not yet know what.

Only the sentence that remained from the dream, clear and unaltered:

Remember, and let remembering change you.

He had tried to outrun those words once. Buried them beneath busyness, beneath silence, beneath the practiced numbness men learn to wear like armor. But dreams do not dissolve when ignored. They wait. They circle back. They arrive when a person has finally grown enough to bear them.

The sea wind crossed his face. Salt on his tongue, and beneath it, the remembered taste of blood.

"I don't know how to do this," he said quietly, not to Noko, not to anyone. Just to the presence within him.

For a moment, there was only the slow rhythm of the tide.

It pulled and returned with steady patience, as if the sea itself were listening. The sound pressed gently against his awareness, not demanding attention, only keeping time. His breath began to follow it. In and out. The boundary between his body and the shoreline softened.

Then came something like an answer, not in words, but in feeling.

A quiet awareness of presence. Of accompaniment. Not a voice, not an image, but the unmistakable sense that he was being held within something larger than himself.

Not alone.

The realization unsettled him and comforted him at once. It loosened something he had kept clenched for years, even as it asked him to remain awake to what followed.

He thought of his father, of the uncompromising distance between them. Of the whale boat. Of the oil. Of the village that whispered survival and sacrifice in the same breath. He thought of lineage not as pride or shame, but as a river that flowed through all who had ever lived inside it.

Una had entered his life not to pull him backward but rather to show him the undercurrent he had always been swimming in without seeing.

Between hunter and hunted.

Between past and future.

Between wound and healing.

He opened his eyes. The horizon brightened. The fishing boats in the harbor creaked and shifted with the tide, ordinary and sacred at once.

Purpose did not arrive as thunder. It arrived as a quiet willingness.

He stood.

The water mirrored the sky, and for an instant, his reflection did not look like only his own. There was something older in it. Something that remembered depths he had never seen with human eyes.

"I will not forget," he whispered.

The ocean answered in its language, a long rolling swell that lifted and released.

Somewhere beneath the surface, old griefs turned and moved, not yet healed, but no longer buried.

He did not know what he would do. But he knew the direction he was facing.

And that, for the first time, was enough.

Chapter Thirteen

"Deckhand"

Days slipped into weeks, and the rhythm of tides became Homer's anchor. Purpose had not yet shaped itself into action, but movement called to him. He found himself drawn more and more to the wharf, to the smell of tar and hemp rope, to the way the harbor always seemed to be both arriving and leaving at once. When a chance came to sign on as a deckhand aboard a small merchant boat, he did not hesitate. Work with his hands felt honest, and the open water offered a kind of listening that the land did not.

He did not announce that he was searching for something. He simply went to sea.

The merchant boat was unremarkable by most measures, sturdy rather than graceful, its planks scarred, its rigging creaking like old bones when the wind stiffened. To Homer, it was beautiful.

He learned to scrub salt-crust from deck boards until the wood shone dark like stain. He became very proficient with how to coil rope so it lay obedient, deck-wise, and how to read the wind from the tilt of a gull's wings. The work was hard, but its simplicity steadied him. There was no pretending at sea; a knot was tied or it wasn't, a sail held or it didn't. The sea accepted no excuses.

The boat ran familiar routes along the New England coast, from Newport to Providence, Providence to Boston, sometimes farther north when cargo and weather allowed. They hauled barrels of whale oil, crates of dry goods, bolts of cloth, smoked fish, hard bread, and cheese. It was unromantic work, the quiet lifeblood of coastal towns, and Homer was grateful for every mile of it.

Boston was different.

The city pressed outward with modern edges. Storefronts stretched block after block. Cobblestones rang beneath carriage wheels. Everything felt louder, denser, swollen with movement. The harbor was crowded with merchant ships and fishing boats, but also with something else, naval vessels resting in the water like sleeping giants.

On his first trip, Homer simply stared.

Grey hulls. Tall masts. Lines of men moving with practiced precision. Flags snapped in the wind like living things. He felt something shift inside him, the way a tide turns without asking permission.

On later trips, he walked closer.

He found himself lingering near the Boston Naval Shipyard, standing shoulder to shoulder with other deckhands and longshoremen who had come just to watch. Sailors passed in pairs and groups, laughing, shouting, hauling bundles of rope or canvas over their shoulders.

One afternoon, a sailor about his age noticed Homer studying the ships.

“First time seeing her?” the sailor asked, nodding toward a moored naval vessel.

“Second,” Homer replied. “Still feels like the first.”

The sailor grinned. “Aye. That’s the way of it. You either fear ‘em or you fall in love with ‘em. Sometimes both.”

Homer hesitated, then asked, “What’s it like. Navy life?”

The sailor leaned against a piling, considering. “Long days. Long nights. Orders you don’t always like. But the world...” He swept his hand toward the horizon. “The world opens.”

Another sailor joined them, adding, “Ports you’ve never heard of. Stars over water so black it feels like you’re floating in the sky. Storms that make you pray, whether you believe in anything at all.”

Homer listened as if to a story he already knew the ending of.

“Can anyone join?” he asked.

“If a man’s sound of body and can learn to follow command,” the first sailor said. “Shipyard office will tell you what’s needed. Papers. Signatures. Maybe a recommendation or two.”

Homer nodded, thanking them, but the conversation followed him long after they walked away.

On later visits, he circled the shipyard with intention. He learned ship names. Watched drills. He began to recognize faces. He did not rush his curiosity. He let it unfold at its own pace, like something that already knew its season.

At night, in the narrow bunk of the merchant boat, he held his journal in the palm of his hand.

The cover and pages smelled faintly of oil and salt.

I think I am meant to go, he wrote.

Not as a flight from those I love, but as a stepping forward into a path they cannot walk with me, one I do not yet fully understand. I am going because something is asking me to serve in a way that only I can, beyond what home can hold.

He paused, the lantern light flickering beside him.

I am afraid to tell them.

Father most of all.

He could see Marcus's face in his mind, the firm line of his jaw, the history behind his eyes, the legacy of a man taught that duty was a weight one carried without complaint. Homer did not doubt his father's strength. He doubted his father's ability to understand why a son might walk a different path.

He will think I am abandoning the family legacy.

He will think I am abandoning him.

He closed his eyes and felt Una's presence stir as a steady undercurrent of knowing.

But my heart is not safe if I stay only to please another man's idea of who I should be, he wrote.

There is something in me that remembers the deep and calls me toward it. If I ignore it, I will become hollow.

He set the pencil down.

Outside, the hull of the ship sighed against the dock as if in agreement.

Weeks passed. Each time the boat returned to Boston, he returned to the shipyard. He spoke with officers, read notices, held the papers in his hands that would formally tie him to the sea. Each time, he half expected certainty to leave him.

It did not.

On the day he finally decided, the choice did not arrive with thunder or speeches. It came like the turning of a tide, quiet and unstoppable.

He stood before the recruitment office, the bustle of the yard alive around him, and felt fear and alignment in the same breath.

Una was with him.

Noko's words were with him.

His own voice, finally steady.

The recruiting officer invited Homer inside his office. Homer stepped forward. The door closed behind him, and another life opened.

What followed did not happen all at once. It unfolded in slow, deliberate steps with forms signed, dates set, promises made. It unfolded in sleepless nights when the ceiling above his bed seemed to drift like sky over open water. It unfolded in the long days that passed between decision and departure, days filled with work, with the rhythms of tide and rope and sail, and with the steady ache of what he had chosen.

Through all of it, Una remained near, like a current beneath the surface of his thoughts. And as the day of departure drew closer, Homer understood that this choice had not been made in isolation. It had been witnessed, carried, and spoken into being through the conversations he had already begun.

Chapter Fourteen

"Black Tear Stone"

Years had passed since Homer had first shared the dream with Noko. Una's presence lingered with him, steady as the tide. After signing his enlistment papers in Boston, he returned to Newport with the weight of the decision tucked inside him like a sealed letter. He found Noko where he had always known he would, near the rocks above the tideline, gathering herbs in the fading light. When she looked up and saw him, her face softened first with relief, then with an open sense of curiosity at the storm she sensed behind his eyes.

They walked together along the familiar stones above the breathing sea. The moon laid its silver road across the water as it had so many nights before. Before he spoke, there was a sense of quiet understanding in silence between them. Noko folded her legs beneath her. Homer let his feet dangle over the dark waves, as he had when he was younger, before the world had grown heavy. He told her about Boston, about the shipyard, about the sailors who spoke of distant ports and wide horizons. He spoke of fear, of excitement, and then, at last, the truth. He had signed.

Noko's breath caught, not in anger, but in startled recognition, as though some prophecy had arrived earlier than expected. Between them, the silence deepened. Homer felt it press against his chest like a tide turning.

He drew in a steady breath. He was ready to say the words aloud.

"I'm leaving," he said quietly.

Noko did not look at him right away. She continued tracing circles in the sand with a small piece of driftwood, as if giving the words time to settle. Then she slowly shifted her gaze toward Homer and studied his face for a long moment, as though reading more than his words. "You are running?" she asked cautiously. It was not an accusation.

Homer nodded. "I don't know how to stay. Not without becoming someone I'm not."

"Leaving where?" she asked.

Homer swallowed with an audible sound. "Newport. The whaleboats. My father." He hesitated, then added, "I'm making my way north, to Boston. I have signed on with the Navy."

That caught her attention. She looked at him then, really looking and searching his face not for certainty, but for truth.

"So you will still sail?"

"Yes," Homer replied. "But not to hunt. Not to take," he paused. "I don't know exactly what I'm running toward… I just know I can't stay."

Noko nodded, as though she had been expecting this answer long before he found the words for it. Noko reached down and brushed her fingers across the sand.

"Sometimes leaving is how we protect what we love," she said. "Including ourselves."

"The ocean has many paths," she added. "Some are loud. Some are quiet. But they all move."

She reached into the small leather pouch at her side and pulled out an obsidian stone she traded a handcrafted basket for. It was smooth, dark, and reflective even in the moonlight. It seemed to hold a quiet weight of purpose. She placed it gently into Homer's palm, her fingers lingering for a moment as if passing on more than just the stone.

"What is it?" he asked.

"Xaga," she said. "Born from fire and water."

Homer turned it over in his hand, surprised by its polished surface.

"Our people have used stones like this for many generations," Noko continued. "Hunters carried it for protection from danger, finding direction from becoming lost in what they had to do to survive. It was believed to absorb harmful spirits, to hold anger and fear so they didn't poison the heart. It protected the family, the hunter, and the balance between taking life and honoring it."

She closed his fingers around the stone.

"This is for you," she said softly. "So you do not forget who you are while you are gone."

Homer felt something tighten in his chest. "This is a very generous gift. It feels like something I do not deserve."

Noko smiled faintly. “It is not about deserving. It is about remembering.”

They sat in silence after that, the sound of waves below filled the space between them. Homer stared out at the open water, the obsidian warm in his hand, the dark surface catching the moonlight in tiny sparkles.

“When I come back,” he said, unsure if it was a promise or a hope, “things will be different.”

Noko did not answer right away. She reached out, brushing a strand of hair from his face, her gaze steady.

“They always are,” she said finally. “For those who walk a long journey.”

Homer leaned closer to Noko, their eyes locking, as he reached for her neck and pulled her until their lips gently touched. An energy raced through their whole bodies illuminating each heart palpitation like their familiar shared breath. One rhythm between two hearts. The ocean seemed to breathe and move with them, as if celebrating. The stars gathered slowly above, circling their stillness like the Milky Way.

Homer traced the edges of the stone, feeling its weight settle into his palm as if it carried the pulse of the ocean itself. He thought of the whales, of the hunt, of the shadow of his father’s expectations looming over him. And yet, within the stone, he found a quiet reassurance with a reminder that even across distance and time, there were forces watching over him, guiding him. He tucked it safely into his pocket, letting its darkness remind him of both the world he came from and the world he was about to step into.

Chapter Fifteen

"Whale Hunter's Legacy"

Mist clung to the docks of the wharf in Newport the following morning, drifting across the creaking wooden planks and the hulls of empty vessels waiting for labor. Homer's stomach churned as he stood near the edge, uniform pressed and polished, his small seabag slung over one shoulder. The village he had grown up in over the past eighteen years, with its ocean-swept streets, weathered houses, and constant scent of salt and fish, felt simultaneously like sanctuary and cage. Every sound drew him backward. The memory returned without mercy, the bloodied hunt, the whale's tail thrashing as life receded, the thick odor of oil, the cries that had followed him into sleep.

Homer tried to fill his father's boots, but every attempt to hunt for whales left his conscience more eroded. He had argued, shouted, and even grabbed his father's harpoon more than once. He recalled his father's damning words of disapproval and the sunken feeling of unmet expectations. He knew he was not becoming heir to the Deep family legacy Marcus had inherited and demanded. But Homer never forgot the way he felt as a young boy, that day had etched itself into his bones, a wound of conscience he could not close.

Standing at the wharf, he reflected on the form of duty he had inherited. His father's will had shaped the household like the steady hands of a master sailor shaping a ship's course. Marcus's duty had been to family, to legacy, to survival, all measured in the provision of harpoons, oil, and profits. Homer's sense of duty had taken a different shape, one that called him toward service beyond the village, toward discipline, toward a reckoning with himself. The weight was familiar, even if the path was not.

The Navy had not been a childhood ambition. Instead, it arrived as an answer to a question Homer could no longer avoid. He could not remain in Newport and become what his father expected, nor could he live without some form of discipline, purpose, and honor. The sea was still in his blood but the harpoon was not. The Navy offered a way to honor the sea without violating it, to serve something larger than himself without surrendering his conscience. Leaving was not abandonment. It was survival.

A glimmer stirred at the edge of his mind, a memory unfolding. He saw Noko, crouched near the tide pool on the cliffs years ago, her dark hair falling across her shoulders as she traced the shapes of crabs and shells, whispering to the creatures as if the ocean itself were listening. We have to respect that, she had said. The words lingered, but beneath them stirred something older, vaster, rising from the sea's endless breath.

Homer slowed his steps. The surf below seemed to speak in pulses rather than sound, and within that rhythm he felt a quiet, watchful, and familiar presence. It was not Noko's voice alone that guided him now, but another current moving through him, ancient and insistent. Una spoke without language, through sensation, through the ache behind his ribs, through the pull that reminded him life was meant to be honored, not mastered.

He thought of the countless nights he had walked the cliffs and beaches, searching for Noko, signaling with stone cairns or symbols in the sand. What he had been reaching for, he realized, was larger than either of them. It was the sacred truth carried by the ocean itself, and now, impossibly, carried within him.

Homer's family gathered behind him, Elizabeth's hands wringing, her eyes glistening with pride and worry. His siblings shifted nervously as they tried to understand their own emotions in an unfamiliar moment. Marcus stood stoic, jaw tight, eyes fixed on his eldest son. There was no warm embrace, no dramatic speeches. Marcus's way was different. He nodded once, a single motion heavy with unspoken meaning. Homer had loved and feared this man all his life, and now he felt the weight of that complicated bond pressing hard against his chest.

"You'll do well," Marcus said finally, voice low, almost reluctant. "Make us proud. Do what's right. Keep your head."

Homer nodded, unable to speak. The words felt like both blessing and command. He stepped aboard the Jollyboat, heart pounding in rhythm with the churning water beneath. The ropes tightened, sails rustled, and the vessel groaned under the weight of its own purpose. The horizon stretched wide and unknowable before him, and for the first time in years, he felt both fear and exhilaration.

He pulled out a small leather journal from his seabag, the one he had carried since his uncompromising estrangement with Marcus. The pages were filled with sketches of whales, notes about tides, and musings about the cliffs and forests he had wandered with Noko, and her insightful guidance. He opened it and wrote:

I leave Newport carrying more than my own ambitions. I carry the ocean in my blood, the lessons of life and death, the memory of grief that is not mine alone. I leave for duty, in a quest for honor, and for a chance to define myself beyond the legacy of harpoons and oil. But I will not forget the creatures of the sea, nor my true friend who taught me to see the balance in all things.

As the Jollyboat cast off and the dock receded, Homer felt the familiar pull of the ocean beneath him, the whispering winds and distant cries of seabirds, and in that moment he understood that his journey had only just begun. The shadow of his father, the weight of legacy, and the call of the sea would follow him always. But, so would Noko, and the quiet knowledge she had instilled. That honor could coexist with compassion, and duty could be guided by ancestral ties.

The world stretched before him, immense and uncharted, yet Homer's heart carried the seed of rebellion, empathy, and an emerging understanding of what it meant to protect rather than destroy. In his palm, the obsidian stone Noko had given him caught the faint glint of the rising sun. It offered a talisman of guidance, protection, and the quiet wisdom of a friend who had seen him when no one else could.

With every furlong that took him away from Newport, he bore the love and the tension of the family he left behind, a legacy both heavy and instructive, one that would haunt him, teach him, and eventually demand a reckoning with the father he both revered and resisted. As the jollyboat's hull cut through the waves, Homer felt the first stirrings of a journey that was entirely his own. This was a voyage toward understanding and toward a self he had yet to discover.

Chapter Sixteen

"A New Compass"

Homer clutched the obsidian stone Noko had pressed into his hand just days before. Its smooth, dark surface was a reminder of her guidance and the quiet strength she had recognized in him. The jollyboat approached Boston Harbor, stretching ahead like a new world with towering masts, crowded docks, and the sharp tang of salt, tar, and iron in the air. With each furlong, the distance from Newport widened, carrying both relief and guilt, the weight of his father's expectations pressing alongside his own budding sense of independence. The stone seemed to pulse faintly in his palm, as if urging him onward, whispering that this voyage was not merely about leaving home, but about discovering who he was becoming.

The jollyboat bumped gently against the wooden docks of the Boston Naval Shipyard, ropes creaking as sailors shouted orders over the clamorous harbor. Homer stepped onto the cobblestones, the salt-and-iron scent of the harbor filling his lungs, and took in the bustling scene. Groups of young men from across the countryside milled about as officers moved with brisk authority, the clatter of cargo and chains echoing off the massive warehouses. He was guided along the pier by a stern instructor, meeting other recruits who shared a mixture of curiosity and trepidation, each sizing up the others as potential allies or rivals.

Soon, they were led across the sprawling naval campus, an organized tangle of training grounds, barracks, and drills, where Homer would spend the coming weeks mastering the discipline of naval life. During this brief period, he was learning the chain of command, daily routines, and the strict protocols that defined service. The air was thick with expectation. Every sharp whistle and shouted order reinforced the seriousness of the life he had chosen.

Then he saw her. Ahead, moored in the harbor, the Pawnee rose above him, a leviathan shaped from wood and steel. Iron bracing and plated sections glinted in the morning sun, bound into a hull of seasoned timber scarred by weather and work. Her masts climbed high, rigging drawn tight and coiled with strength, the whole of her held together like the muscled frame of a giant Trojan Horse. She was a vessel built for war, part craft, part machine, carrying the weight of an older world into a new one.

Homer's chest tightened at the sight of her, she was both intimidating and magnificent. The ship would become home, teacher, proving ground, and the vessel that would carry him farther from the life of hunts and bloodied seas. It was here he would first meet the ship's Captain, Indiana Adams. His commanding presence promised rigor and guidance that would shape the first chapter of Homer's life beyond Newport.

As the large ship set sail from the port, Captain Adams moved with authority across the deck, commanding the crew with crisp efficiency. Orders were given, bunks assigned, routines set for the young sailors. Homer drew a steady breath, easing the churn of excitement and unease in his stomach. Newport, with its ocean-swept streets, weathered homes, and the memory of bloodied hunts, receded behind him. Every wave and gull's cry tugged at the past he had left. Love. Conflict. The unspoken rebellion against his father's legacy, held at a widening distance.

Homer swallowed hard and turned toward the young man who would share his narrow quarters. He fought to gather himself as he approached his new bunkmate. Robert Brown hailed from Salem, Massachusetts, his speech marked by a rhythmic, confident cadence.

Like Homer, Robert had joined the Navy both as an escape and as a path to opportunities beyond the family trade. Trained by his father to repair looms and other large equipment, Robert was technically skilled and mechanically proficient, traits that would serve him well in the rigors of naval life.

Robert's family came from a Black American household free from the shadow of slavery that still lingered in parts of the nation. The Browns had built and operated a modest textile business specializing in cotton goods through a legacy of hard work and perseverance spanning generations.

In their shared quarters, the two unpacked their modest belongings and exchanged cautious stories of home, quickly discovering a quiet kinship rooted in their common desire for freedom, adventure, and self-determination. Homer spoke of Newport, hunting boats, and a legacy he had never truly chosen. Robert confessed that his parents were pressing him toward an arranged marriage with a wealthy family, while his heart leaned toward someone from simpler means. Expectation, they both realized, wore many faces.

They reminded each other to meet on deck in an hour for a tour of the ship that would become their home, a vessel where they would grow and be tested, transforming from boys into men.

Homer retrieved the letter Noko had written to him, her familiar handwriting warming his heart. She remained his anchor, a quiet presence of understanding and steadiness. Their first kiss beneath the stars lingered with him, a sweetness edged with distance. Some connections, he sensed, endured even across oceans and duty.

He allowed himself a small smile, though uncertainty pressed at its edges. He wondered, briefly, what shape their connection might take if time and distance were kind. They came from different worlds. That much was clear. What lay between those worlds did not need to be examined yet.

He folded the thought away as he had folded the letter, careful not to damage it by handling it too soon. The future would arrive on its own terms. For now, the ship around him demanded attention. Wood, iron, rope, and order. A life already in motion.

Robert's quiet concerns echoed in him as well, different in form but familiar in weight. Each man aboard carried something unseen. Expectations set long before choice was offered. Homer understood then that duty followed everyone, whether drawn by blood, by tradition, or by the call of something larger than oneself.

The tour of the ship left Homer in awe. Cannons. Rigging. Compass rooms. Quarters. The Pawnee felt alive and immense. Her scale and order made one truth unmistakable. Responsibility now governed every breath. It moved through the ship like a current, boys settling into purpose, fear sharpening into focus.

The mess hall offered a different lesson. It rang with laughter and the clatter of tin, thick with the smell of gravy-covered meat, bland vegetables, and warm milk. Camaraderie rose easily among the young men, stitched together by shared uncertainty. Talk drifted toward distant ports, imagined lovers, and the trials ahead. Beneath the noise lived a quieter understanding. War could come. When it did, none of them would remain unchanged. Homer felt the weight of accountability settle on him for the first time, familiar in its shape, mirroring the lessons of duty and restraint carried from his father's hand.

That night, exhausted, Homer and the others laid out their uniforms with care, smoothing creases, aligning buttons, committing orders to memory. 0600 wake-up. 0630 mess. The numbers settled into him with the weight of law. Lantern light dimmed as voices fell quiet, boots were stowed, and the ship eased into its night rhythm, timbers ticking softly as they cooled.

Homer lay back in his narrow bunk and closed his fingers around the obsidian stone. Its surface was smooth and cool at first, then slowly warmed against his palm. He traced its contours without thought, letting the shape steady him. Noko's teachings returned not as words, but as presence. A reverence for life that required no defense. An attention to rhythm learned by watching tides rather than measuring them. The patience to remain still long enough for meaning to reveal itself.

The ship's motion rocked him gently. Breath slowed. The weight of the day loosened its hold. Sleep arrived without announcement.

He was standing once more on the cliffs above Newport. The ocean spread wide below, dark and breathing. Noko walked beside him, close enough that he felt her without turning. The wind moved through them both, carrying the salt and the sound of distant water, and for a moment there was no ship, no orders, no distance at all. Only the steady ground beneath his feet and the vast listening sea before them.

"Can you hear that?" Noko asked in his dream.

"I… I only hear the ocean," Homer replied, uncertain.

“Slow your breath. Release your thoughts. Listen.” Her voice was calm, insistent, and ancient, as if carrying the wisdom of generations.

As he obeyed, the songs of whales filled his mind. What had been a single vast symphony separated into layers, low tones rising first, then others answering from far away, long and resonant, bending through water and distance. The sound moved through him rather than toward him, pressing into bone and breath, a living melody of life and survival.

Whales sang across distances the human mind could barely hold. Mourning songs. Traveling songs. Warnings pulsing through saltwater. Some voices held steady while others broke and fell away. Pods passed through one another in sound alone, calls overlapping, diverging, returning. Some sang. Some cried. Each call settled deep within him.

The sea itself seemed to listen. Homer felt the weight of it gather inside him, not as thought, but as recognition, a knowing carried in rhythm and vibration, of balance, protection, and the fragile threads binding all life together.

He reached out to touch what seemed so real.

“Wake up, time to get up!” Robert’s voice shattered the dream.

Homer opened his eyes to the dim lantern light of the quarters, the ship still and breathing around him. His heart raced from the lingering dream, then steadied as his fingers closed around the obsidian stone, now warm from his palm. The narrow bunk creaked softly with the movement of others rising nearby. Somewhere down the passage, boots struck wood. A voice called an order, low and practiced.

Two currents pulled within him, neither willing to give way. One carried the weight of duty, routine, and the discipline that would soon shape his days. The other moved more quietly, carried in memory and sound, in the echo of whale song that had not fully released him. He lay still for a moment longer, letting both exist without forcing a choice.

Today would bring training, correction, and the first full measure of life aboard the ship. He knew that much. Yet beneath the coming hours ran a steadier thread. The presence of Noko. The listening sea. The understanding that what he carried could not be stripped away by distance or command.

Homer swung his legs from the bunk and rose with the others. The stone disappeared into his pocket, close to his body. Whatever lay ahead, he would meet it carrying more than orders alone.

He stepped forward into the unknown.

Chapter Seventeen

"Duty and Dreams"

After a few weeks on the ship, Homer had assimilated quite comfortably into the rhythm of Navy life. He and Robert were part of the deck cleaning crew along with several other "squids." They also served as cabin boys who carried out tasks and delivered messages for the ranking officers. They jokingly called themselves "The Pollywogs," which seemed analogous with their position in the chain of command. The name stuck because it fit.

They were constantly being ordered to go do this, go do that, usually followed by an urgent call to move "on the double." Buckets were hauled, decks scrubbed, and lines coiled and recoiled until the work began to settle into muscle memory. The hierarchy made itself known quickly, who spoke, who waited, who moved without being asked. Life in the Navy thus far suited young Homer well enough, keeping him occupied enough to leave little room for homesickness. By the time he reached his bunk at night, there were only a few minutes for writing in his journal and talking quietly with Robert before exhaustion took them both. Morning came, and the routine took hold again.

Although the days could feel monotonous at times, they were

never quite the same. Each brought a different task, a shared joke passed down the line, or a brief exchange that lingered just long enough to keep boredom at bay.

Sleep, however, held something else entirely.

Night after night, Homer slipped into a depth that felt heavier than rest. His body surrendered quickly, but his mind did not drift. It sank. The world narrowed, sound thickened, and sensation gathered with an unfamiliar gravity. These were not dreams that dissolved with waking. They arrived with shape and weight, lingering long enough to unsettle him.

One night, he found himself on watch atop the deck, moving quietly beneath a full moon that laid its pale reflection across the water. The ship was still. No footsteps. No voices. The air felt held, as though the night itself were listening.

From below came the voices of whales.

At first, the sounds were distant, low vibrations carried across the surface. Then they rose, layered and urgent. A pod broke the water nearby, their bodies churning as their calls shifted from warning into something closer to grief. The sea answered them, restless and alive.

One older female lifted higher than the rest.

Her eyes met his.

The gaze struck with force, ancient and heavy with knowing. Grief lived there, but so did recognition. Homer felt her attention settle fully upon him, as though the space between them had closed. No words passed. None were needed. The meaning pressed into him directly, bypassing thought, settling deep within his chest.

She was speaking to him.

And somehow she knew him.

From a life he could not remember.

Homer woke with a sharp intake of breath, his heart pounding, the sheets damp with cold sweat beneath where his head lay. For a moment, he was unsure whether he was still on watch or lying in his bunk below deck. The boundary between dream and waking had thinned to something fragile, easily crossed. This had happened before.

He lay still, listening. The ship hummed softly around him, wood and iron moving together in familiar rhythms. The dream did not release him. It lingered in his body, heavy and close, like seawater trapped in his lungs. He told himself it had only been a dream, even as questions pressed in, uninvited and insistent.

Why does this keep happening to me?

Why do they seem so real?

He could remember the whales clearly, their cries echoing through his body, vibrating through bone and breath, the unblinking gaze of the older female fixed on him with an intensity that refused to fade. Her presence stayed with him even after waking, as if she had not remained behind in the dream but followed him across the threshold. What he could not remember was the passage of time itself. The moment of standing on deck dissolved without warning, and the next thing he knew he was waking in his bunk, the space between those moments missing, unreachable. Time seemed to bend inward, folding over itself, and his sense of reality wavered, as though something essential had been interrupted before it could complete its course.

Beneath that disorientation, guilt waited.

It pressed quietly but persistently, shaping the way the memories returned, determining which images rose and which remained submerged. He could not understand why these night visions arrived with such force, why they felt so immediate, so insistent, and so saturated with whales. Again and again his thoughts circled back to the countless lives taken at sea, the hunts led by Captain Marcus, the kills carried out by crews who followed orders without pause, and the moments when he himself had stood among them, silent and compliant. The accumulation of it settled heavily in his chest, tightening his breath.

He remembered his first kill with uncomfortable clarity. The surge of pride. The recoil of revulsion. The way the ocean had seemed to hold its breath in the instant after. What he had believed buried began to rise again, slow and unrelenting. Those old emotions slipped back into his waking thoughts and his dreams alike, threading themselves through his inner life, refusing to remain quiet. What he had once pushed aside was returning now with intention, asking to be faced. And somewhere beneath the guilt and confusion, he sensed that the whales in his dreams were not merely memories, but messengers, carrying something he had not yet found the courage to name.

During the day, those memories resurfaced most often when he worked alone. In the quiet spaces between tasks, they returned without warning, slipping into his thoughts before he could redirect them. Homer, a deep thinker by his own admission, reminded himself to begin replacing the pull of solitude and melancholy with steadier ground. He turned his focus toward the good in his life, toward the choice he had made to leave the familiarity of his village and step away from a future he could not accept.

He returned often to thoughts of Noko. Her face came to him

with quiet clarity, followed by the sound of her voice and the warmth of her affection. Remembering her steadied him. She anchored his thoughts in a life shaped by care rather than blood and harpoons, offering a sense of direction that felt chosen rather than inherited.

Conversations with Robert brought Homer a quiet sense of relief, the reassurance that he was not alone in carrying the unspoken weight that came with belonging to a family shaped by rigid views and heavy expectations. In the dim hours below deck, their talks unfolded easily, drifting from fears to ambitions, from doubts to moments of laughter that arrived without effort and eased something tight in the chest. Those exchanges became an anchor for Homer, steadying him during a season when uncertainty pressed in from all sides and answers felt distant.

He could not imagine a bunkmate better suited to that moment in his life. Robert listened without judgment, spoke with care, and offered sincerity without pretense, a presence that required nothing more than honesty in return.

When Robert opened up about his own strained relationship with his father, Homer met him with empathy and careful counsel, recognizing familiar patterns in his friend's struggle. Robert, too, was navigating new and complicated terrain, carrying the weight of love for a girl back home and the frustration that came with her parents' refusal to see him as worthy of their daughter's future. The situation weighed heavily on Robert, and Homer felt a deep ache for him, knowing his friend's character, loyalty, and quiet strength would make him a gift to any family willing to see beyond appearances or circumstance.

Their friendship became something essential, a steadying presence amid the unfamiliar routines of ship life and the emotional undercurrents neither man could fully name. In one another, they found balance, a place where doubts could surface without fear and where mutual understanding softened the sharp edges of isolation. Together, they held one another upright, not through grand gestures, but through the simple, sustaining act of being seen and heard.

But Robert also noticed something else happening to Homer.

At night, the ship no longer slept quietly around him. Low sounds would rise from Homer's bunk, strained breaths and murmured words shaped by distress he could not remember in the morning. At first, Robert thought it was simply exhaustion working its way out, the mind unburdening itself after long days at sea. But the sounds returned again and again, carrying a tone that felt deeper than ordinary dreaming.

When it became too much, Robert would reach across the narrow space between them and wake him gently, speaking his name until Homer surfaced. "It's only a dream," he would say softly, anchoring him back to the present. Homer would jolt awake, disoriented for a moment, his eyes searching the dark before recognition settled in. Embarrassment followed quickly, a flush of self-consciousness, but it was always accompanied by quiet gratitude. He never said much afterward, only nodded and lay still until sleep returned.

Yet Homer knew these visions were not merely the restless imaginings of an overtired mind. They carried a weight that lingered long after waking, pressing against him during the day with an intensity he could not shake. The images felt older than memory, rising with a force that bypassed thought and went straight to the body. It was as if something long submerged was pushing upward, insisting on being felt, refusing to retreat.

The ocean had begun speaking to him.

And for the first time, Homer no longer knew how to turn away.

Chapter Eighteen

"The Lizard and The Snake"

The nights grew stranger.

Homer slipped with ease into dreams that seemed to carry their own gravity, as if sleep itself had weight and direction. Again and again he awoke with his lungs burning, the sharp panic of air denied, as though he had failed to reach the surface of the water in time. Each return to waking came with the same reflex, a sudden gasp, a hand pressed instinctively to his chest, the echo of depth still clinging to his body.

On one such night, he surfaced abruptly from a startling dream, caught in the narrow twilight between sleep and awareness. His mind drifted there, unmoored and restless, unable to settle back into rest, unable to fully wake. An image lingered just beyond understanding, circling him with quiet insistence.

A snake and a lizard, locked together, chasing each other endlessly by the tail.

In the dream, Homer was the monitor lizard, muscles coiled tight as he grappled with the serpent. He clamped down on the tail and tried to consume it, but the effort yielded nothing. The snake twisted and resisted, the struggle repeating itself without progress. Time stretched. Strength drained. The task consumed him even as it refused to be completed.

Then a familiar voice entered the dream, steady and unmistakable.

"Start with the head rather than the tail."

Homer shifted his grip. The moment he seized the serpent by its head, the resistance vanished. He crushed it with ease and gobbled it whole. The struggle ended as suddenly as it had begun.

Homer jolted awake, shaken by the darkness of the scene and the force of the instruction. He felt uneasy as it lingered, evoking a deep and troubling significance both haunting and symbolic, although he could not yet understand its meaning.

Why am I dreaming such darkness?

Despite his exhaustion, sleep did not return easily that night.

That image resurfaced alongside his uncle's story of Captain Marcus's first whale kill, told years later in a low voice meant for no one else. Thad had once confided that Marcus, still young then, returned from that hunt stunned, altered in a way that did not pass. He came home quieter. Slower. Something in him had shifted and never quite found its way back.

Marcus never spoke of it to Homer. He never spoke of tears. But Thad had seen them. He had seen the grief his brother tried to bury beneath discipline and duty, beneath the hard work of providing and the silence expected of men who did not look back.

Sharing the story had bound Homer and his uncle together, not through agreement, but through restraint. They carried it quietly. Captain Marcus would have been furious to know that any trace of vulnerability had been spoken aloud. Yet Homer felt no sense of betrayal in knowing it. He felt only empathy. What others might have called weakness, Homer recognized as fracture. A moment that split a life into before and after.

His own struggle with memory did not distance him from his father. It drew him closer. It humanized him. It revealed the man beneath the captain, the son beneath the authority, the cost paid long before Homer ever entered the world.

One moment had been enough.

What began as survival hardened into repetition. Kill layered upon kill. Feeling calcified into callousness until it no longer softened anything it touched.

Compartmentalizing emotion was not a trait Homer inherited from his father. His memories refused burial. The whales he had been instructed to kill followed him into sleep, their bodies and voices returning without permission. They did not fade with time. They accumulated.

Now his father's past threaded itself through those nights as well. Stories once spoken in confidence seeped into his dreams until they merged with his own experience. The boundary between inherited memory and lived action collapsed, pressing against him with an urgency he could not ignore.

Then the songs began.

Again and again, whales cried out in his dreams, their voices rising and falling in patterns that felt both ancient and unfinished. Something was forming beneath the repetition. Something was asking to be recognized.

Then came another dream beneath the moonlight.

Like before, the dream started with Homer returning to the top deck for his duty as night watch. The ship moved gently beneath his feet. While standing his post, he heard moans and cries from the ocean. He stepped to the rail and looked toward the glimmer of water illuminated by the full moon. Pods of whales churned the surface, their bodies colliding and rolling in panic.

This time, the dream lasted long enough to allow Homer to see a small boat carrying three hunters. Homer's heart jolted at first as he thought he saw himself in the boat. Suddenly clarity struck like a wave.

It wasn't him.

It was his father.

Harpoons were raised in each of their hands. Though their voices were drowned out by the screams of the whales, he knew they were already on the attack. The baby whale was helpless as she looked to her mother for guidance, while an elderly whale was in the back trying to lead them all out of danger, but to no avail.

Homer's heart began to beat strong enough for him to hear it thumping from his chest, as he winced with what he saw next. The baby whale had been harpooned and was struggling to get loose when the other two hunters pierced its body with their spears, as well.

In an instant, she was gone.

Homer felt the mother's pain as if it were his own, her scream tearing through the night as she watched her baby die. The sound split something open in him. The moonlight shifted, settling into the eyes of the grandmother, whose sorrow felt guttural and permanent.

And suddenly, undeniably, he knew their names.

The whale who had been reaching him through his dreams was Astra. She was the mother of Una. The grandmother of Kai. These were the whales from Captain Marcus's first hunt, from the stories his uncle had told him in guarded tones. They were playing out in his dreams.

The story was no longer being told.

It was unfolding.

Homer woke in a cold sweat, breath shallow, the names still ringing inside him. He sat upright without thinking, careful not to disturb Robert, and reached for his journal. By lamplight he wrote quickly, his hand struggling to keep pace with what memory had delivered. The sequence made sense as it took shape on the page, every image falling into place, except for one unyielding fact.

His uncle had never known their names.

To Thad, they had been whales. Part of the work. Part of the hunt. Nothing more. Yet Homer knew them. Not as abstractions, but as beings recognized. The connection settled deepest with Una, immediate and undeniable, as if it had always been waiting for him to remember.

Whether the dreams belonged to past or present, imagination or visitation, no longer mattered.

They had crossed into something more.

Chapter Nineteen

"What the Water Remembers"

The dreams returned, familiar yet still overwhelming, like a tide that knew his name. Moonlight washed over the water in a pale silver sheet, and the whales surfaced beneath it as though rising from another world. The cries were no longer simply heard. They were felt inside muscle and marrow, echoing in places language could not reach.

Astra rose first. She moved with the quiet authority of a mother whose body knew both love and loss, carrying grief the way the sea carries salt, not as a burden but as something inseparable from its nature. The ache of what had been taken lived within her muscle and memory, shaping every movement, every sound she released into the water.

Kai lingered nearby, still young, her curiosity untempered by understanding. She watched the world with wide attention, sensing its beauty even as its cruelty brushed against her for the first time. She did not yet know how to hold both at once, only that they existed together, tangled and unresolved.

Una remained behind them, older and deliberate, her presence steady and guiding. She carried history beneath her skin the way the ocean carries its paths, etched through time by repetition and endurance. Old scars marked her not as wounds, but as records of survival, maps of where she had been and what she had endured.

Within this shared expanse, Astra's awareness sharpened.

She no longer saw Homer simply as the human who dreamed of them, nor as a distant observer reaching across worlds. She saw him as the one who carried Una alongside him. Their spirits traveled the same current, two forms shaped differently but drawn forward by the same motion. Una's presence moved through him quietly, not as something borrowed or imposed, but as something joined. It lived in his breath, his instincts, the unspoken pull that guided him even when he did not yet understand its source.

Astra recognized the bond with the certainty of the ocean's tides. The mother and the man were bound, moving together toward something still forming, a convergence neither could yet name, but both were already walking toward.

Homer felt their grief travel through him and settle in his heart as if it belonged there, as if it had been waiting for him to finally feel it. The boundaries between whale and human blurred. He could no longer tell whether he was watching them, or whether he was inside them through their memories, their blood, their song. The ocean itself seemed to hold memory the way bodies hold the cycle of breath: entering, leaving, returning again, never quite gone.

He no longer resisted the visions. He let them pass through like water moving around stone.

He understood now that his life and theirs had entangled long before his birth. His father's hands, the same hands that once lifted him as an infant, had destroyed another mother's child. That truth no longer sat outside him as fact. It lived within him as feeling. Pain moved in circles across generations, never fully disappearing, only changing form, carried like tides, inherited like names.

He did not feel hunted by the dreams anymore.

He felt called.

Later that night, he wrote again, slowly this time, as though each word required respect, as though the page itself could be wounded. He sensed that these visions were not merely about whales or memory or guilt, they were about who he was becoming when no one else was watching. The ship creaked softly around him, a wooden heartbeat. Somewhere beyond it, beneath the same sky, Noko slept unknowingly while he carried something new inside him: a weight and a vow.

He would not become what Marcus had become.

He would not pass the wound forward.

The ocean had borne witness. Now it was asking him to choose.

Astra's knowing moved through him like a current: she saw Una beside him, not gone, not lost, but walking with him. Una's curiosity brushed him like a question: Will it be different with you? Una's presence remained steady behind them both, keeper of stories older than ships, older than gunpowder, older than men who believed the world existed only to be taken.

For the first time, he understood that the voices in his dreams were not crying out only for the past.

They were asking what he would do next.

The ship rocked gently beneath him as dawn began to thin the darkness. The visions dissolved slowly, without violence, like the soft retreat of a tide, leaving sea foam behind. Homer lay still and listened to the creak of the hull, the restless murmurs of sailors waking, the ordinary sounds of men who had never heard whales sing in their sleep. He touched the page where he had written the night before and felt fearless direction.

The voice of the ocean had asked him to choose. The choosing would not happen in the dreamworld, it would happen in daylight.

Beyond the porthole, the outline of land waited, rooftops pressed close together, chimneys already breathing smoke into the morning air. The smell of cooked food carried across the water, bread and fat and something burnt, drifting outward from streets not yet fully awake. The harbor stirred with early movement, small boats crossing paths, dock lines creaking, voices calling out with practiced impatience.

For months his world had been water and sky, governed by wind, current, and the slow honesty of distance. On shore there would be crowds and taverns, laughter thick with drink, letters folded and unfolded until their meaning thinned. There would be noise enough to drown out anything that spoke softly, anything that asked rather than demanded.

He wondered if the voices would follow him ashore.

He wondered if he would listen.

When the sun finally broke over the horizon, Newburyport drew nearer, ordinary and alive, as the ship moved toward harbor. The Pawnee would be docking by afternoon. The men were already speaking of ale, women, and streets.

Homer rose with the others, the vow still steady inside him. He did not yet know that the shore would bring its own currents.

Chapter Twenty

"First Port of Call"

"Man the rails! Stand by to dock!" a voice bellowed from the quarterdeck.

Lines were coiled, boots struck the deck in quick rhythm, and men hurried to their stations as the harbor grew larger ahead of them. The ship leaned toward land as if it, too, were impatient. After three months at sea, the promise of solid ground sent a restless energy racing through the crew. Robert grinned at Homer, clapping him on the shoulder before moving to his post. Homer worked beside him with practiced efficiency, yet beneath the noise and shouted orders, the echo of last night's dreams still pulsed quietly through his chest.

The mood aboard the ship shifted the moment land came into view. There was a palpable sense of excitement among the crew as it would be their first visit to a port.

"Feels strange to see land again, doesn't it?" Robert said, squinting toward the coastline as the ship crept into the harbor.

"Strange," Homer answered, though the word barely held all that he felt.

Robert laughed, slapping his thigh. "Three days ashore with some home-cooked food, real beds, maybe even music with a lady on my arm. That's all I need." Homer could not help but grin at his bunkmate's enthusiasm.

They finished packing the few belongings they would carry off the ship, surrounded by the easy banter of sailors moving around them as the final routines of the voyage unfolded. Homer and Robert completed their tasks and tidied their bunk, leaving the small space bare and orderly. Land waited only hours away. Newburyport promised noise and rest after three months at sea, and for Robert it meant familiar ground, with Boston only a short train ride beyond.

Robert urged Homer to come along with him, eager for the comfort of streets, voices, and the pull of home. Homer smiled and listened, grateful for the invitation, but chose to remain nearby. He felt the need to write, to wander, to give shape to the thoughts and dreams that still moved through him. Though he stood among packed crates and coiled rope, part of his mind remained submerged, drawn by a quiet pull that did not belong to land at all.

Robert slung his bag over his shoulder and bumped Homer lightly with his elbow. "Three days," he said, grinning. "Three whole days without a bell, a deck, or a captain's glare. You sure you won't come to Boston? My mother will feed you until you forget the ship exists."

Homer laughed, but the sound came out softer than he intended. "Another time. There's something I've got to figure out first."

Robert studied him for a moment, expression sobering. "The dreams again?"

Homer hesitated, then nodded. "They're not just dreams anymore. They feel… borrowed. Like they belong to someone else and landed in me by mistake."

"Or not by mistake," Robert replied gently, then clapped him on the back before turning away toward the gangplank. "Find whatever it is you're looking for, Deep."

The dock spread out before Homer like a new page, filled with shouts of crewmen, ropes slapping wood, gulls wheeling overhead, and the mingled scents of tar, brine, and bread drifting in from town. Beneath it all, the echo of whale-song tugged at him faintly, as though the ocean still had him by the sleeve. He walked inland with the steady gait of a man accustomed to rolling decks, unsure where to begin. A library, perhaps. Or a bookseller who did not flinch at the word visions. He imagined asking for help and almost laughed. *Excuse me, sir, where might I find the section on dreams that do not feel like my own?*

The town unfolded around him as he walked the cobblestone streets, passing houses with shuttered windows, and laundry breathing in the wind. The day slipped by in small conversations and fruitless searches. In one narrow shop, a bookseller listened politely as Homer spoke of dreams that lingered past waking. The gentleman then cleared his throat and suggested a sermon pamphlet. No one had a name for what he was searching for. By late afternoon, with the light turning amber and his thoughts heavy, he pushed open the door of a small tavern, lured by warmth and the promise of forgetting for a while. The room smelled of woodsmoke and ale. Laughter rose and fell like waves.

That was when he saw her.

She wove between tables with a practiced ease, strawberry-blonde hair gathered loosely back, voice low and slightly raspy, every word edged with humor. Men twice her age leaned toward her as though drawn by gravity, and she deflected them with quick wit and a raised brow as easily as sidestepping a careless hand. She can hold a room the way a helmsman holds a ship, Homer thought, surprised by the sudden flutter in his chest. He realized how long it had been since he had spoken with a woman who was not part of his family or Noko.

She glanced at him only once, sharp and assessing, then looked away again, and he found himself staying in his seat for reasons that had nothing to do with ale. A voice from behind the counter called, "Elsea, in the kitchen real quick," and she disappeared through the swinging door. Homer stared at the empty space she had left, smiled despite himself, and settled in as the afternoon lengthened, waiting without admitting, even to himself, that he was waiting.

His moment finally came when she set another ale in front of him, unasked, casual, almost conspiratorial, and said, "You look like you could use something more than drink. Would you like some food while you're here?"

The question startled him from his thoughts. "Sure," he said too quickly, then softened it. "Whatever you have in the way of soup."

Elsea nodded. "Fine. It'll be just a few minutes," she replied, already turning, her apron swaying as she disappeared into the kitchen.

Homer's palms felt damp. He tried to assemble topics in his mind, anything to sound less foolish than he felt, but every idea scattered as soon as he reached for it. He stared into the ripples of his ale as though it might offer lines of dialogue along its surface.

She returned sooner than he was ready, setting a large metal bowl of steaming soup before him, along with a thick hunk of bread, a napkin, and a spoon arranged with practiced grace. "Here you are."

"Thank you kindly," Homer said, forcing his voice into steadiness.

Elsea leaned one elbow on the edge of the table, studying him with open curiosity. "So then, what brings you to our quaint little town?"

"We dropped anchor here for the next few days," he replied.

Her attention moved briefly to the harbor beyond the window, then settled back on him. "Oh, so you're a Navy man?" she said, as though the conclusion had formed long before the question, drawn from his stance, his worn clothes, and the way his eyes tracked the space around him.

"Yes," he said. "I have been for nearly one hundred days now. This is our first stop at a port."

"Welcome, then," Elsea replied, and there was something sincere in it, more than politeness, a recognition of distance traveled and things left unsaid.

He took a spoonful of the soup. Heat rose through him, fragrant and familiar in a way that burned a little. "This is very good," he said, almost embarrassed by the earnestness in his own voice. "I haven't had anything close to a home-cooked meal since I left months ago. Please tell the chef thank you."

He immediately second-guessed it as maybe being a little too formal, too stiff, or too boyish, and the thought flashed across his face. She caught it, of course, and offered him a half smile that held both humor and kindness.

"My mother's the cook," she said. "I'll tell her a Navy man approves."

He looked up at her then, meeting her eyes for a moment that lingered longer than politeness required. Something softened in his shoulders.

She straightened to go back to work, then paused. “You look like someone with too many thoughts for just one bowl of soup,” she added lightly. “If you’re staying a while, I get off at sundown.”

And with that she slipped back into the hum of the tavern with all the voices, tankards, the scrape of boots on wooden floors in the background. This left Homer with warmth in his chest that was not only from the broth but with a sudden awareness of how long it had been since he had wanted to stay anywhere at all.

Moments passed when Homer looked up and saw Elsea approaching with another ale, his nerves making his chest tighten slightly. “I don’t believe we’ve been formally introduced,” he said, trying to sound composed. “I’m Homer.”

Elsea paused, arching an eyebrow, then smiled. “Elsea,” she replied, brushing back a strand of strawberry-blonde hair.

Homer giggled, unable to help himself. “I already knew your name,” he admitted. “I overheard your mother call you from the kitchen a moment ago.”

Elsea laughed lightly, a musical sound that made Homer’s stomach flutter. “Caught me, then,” she said. “Well, if you’d like, I can sit and chat once I’m finished here.”

“I’d like that very much,” Homer said, settling into his seat, feeling the warmth of the tavern around him, the smells of stew and ale, and the soft murmur of other patrons.

Elsea scurried off to finish her rounds with each table, chatting with patrons and fending off advances with sharp humor, her strawberry-blonde hair catching the firelight. Homer watched innocently with curiosity. She laughed at sailors' bad jokes, rolling her eyes just enough to tease without offense.

As Homer finished his meal and ale, a warm glow settled over him, the combination of food, beer, and the gentle sway of the ship's motion still felt in his feet. He felt talkative, but reminded himself to pace the conversation.

“Have you lived in this town all your life?” Homer asked.

“Yes,” she replied, balancing a tray with effortless grace. “This is my hometown, and our family runs the inn. I also attend the university.”

Homer nodded, intrigued. It had been months since he had been this close to a woman in a casual setting, nevermind a university student with the poise and wit she carried.

“You must see the same view of the sea every day. Maybe it's different each morning with the change of the tides and seasons?” Homer ventured.

Elsea tilted her head, considering. “Aye. The tides change, the winds shift, and sometimes it surprises you. Like people, I suppose.”

Homer smiled. “You mean people are like the ocean? Constantly moving, impossible to pin down?”

She gave a half-smile, brushing a strand of hair behind her ear. “Exactly. Some are calm, some are fierce. And some you just watch, hoping they don't capsize.”

The atmosphere was relaxing and the conversation with Elsea continued lightly. Homer discovered shared ties to the ocean, a fascination with its mysteries, and a reverence for its rhythms. Her family was steeped in learning, yet grounded in practical work at the inn. Her father was a professor at the university, and her mom taught at the local elementary school when she was not running the tavern. Elsea's entire family helped out with the family business, a balance he found quite admirable. When he finally secured a room for the night, he wanted to ask if she would be there tomorrow but couldn't muster up the words, so he thought it best to leave well enough alone.

Homer carried his knapsack and journal upstairs to his room, the wood creaking softly beneath his boots. He settled at the small desk, candlelight flickering across the pages as he spent the next hours reading and writing, tracing the shapes of his thoughts in ink. After washing up, he blew out the candle and climbed into bed, the warmth from the ale still buzzing through him. The crackle from the fireplace and the distant sound of waves crashing ashore reminded him of the ocean's rhythm, and soon he found a delicate balance between wakefulness and sleep.

Before long, he was adrift in a familiar fog, walking the deck of the ship under a moonlight that glimmered on the black waves. This time, however, he stepped into a small boat moored at the wharf, the mist curling around him like smoke, and the distant cries of the whales weaving through the night air. He was aware of his body beneath the blanket of sleep, half-conscious in his room, yet wholly present in the dream. Thoughts slowed as he allowed himself to drift, letting the ocean guide him deeper into the vision.

The cries were no longer distant, they called to him, vibrant and insistent. Homer moved toward the edge of the pier, fog lifting just enough to reveal the dark shapes dancing in the water. The whales frolicked and splashed, their movements brimming with life and joy. He realized with awe that he could understand their rhythms, the playful arcs of water, the quiet harmonies that resonated in his chest. Though he had not left the wharf in body, his mind was fully immersed in their world. The pod had accepted him, and he felt it like a pulse through his very being. Hours seemed to pass in the timeless space of the dream, yet when he woke briefly to use the restroom, only thirty minutes had elapsed. The scent of the blown-out candle lingered in the air, anchoring him to the present.

Grabbing his journal, Homer relit the candle and began to record the night's vision. He read aloud from a previous entry, letting the words echo in the quiet room:

"I was on night watch or so I thought I was. And, I once again heard the sounds of the whales. This time it was a harmonious cry from the entire pod, as if they were calling out for help. Was it me they were calling to? Or was I the only one who could hear? Do whales always cry? And if there are no witnesses to their call, why do they make it? Would it be foolish to believe they are speaking to me? I can't help but take the emotions I feel from the sounds to heart; these interactions must mean something. I feel their pain through my dreams, and I want to help. But how?"

As he wrote the account of his latest dream, his mind wobbled between the images on the page and the memory of Elsea, her laughter, her warm gaze. He chastised himself for thinking too much of her, reminding himself that she was simply an acquaintance, and yet he felt gratitude for her presence in his thoughts. He continued documenting the whales' calls, the swell of emotion, and the strange clarity he felt within the dream.

Sleep and reality blurred further as he wrote. The visions were becoming a part of his waking hours, intruding in the quiet moments of the day, leaving him fatigued but restless with curiosity. More than once, he was snapped from a daydream by Robert's voice. "Deep, are you okay?" Homer would murmur in response, "Aye, shipshape," grateful for the anchor of friendship in the midst of his wandering mind.

Finally, he set down his pen with thoughts drifting in of Noko and how she would ease the weight of his dreams with a sense of understanding all the possible meanings they bore. He blew out the candle and let himself sink fully into sleep, the rhythm of the ocean and the voices of the whales carrying him toward unknown depths.

Chapter Twenty-One

"Elsea"

Homer opened his eyes and lay still for a moment, orienting himself to the quiet solidity of the room. No rushing water. No distant cries. He had grown accustomed to waking from dreams that clung to him like fog, but this morning felt different, lighter and grounded. For the first time in a long while, he felt rested. The sea was quiet this morning, as if granting him permission to be fully present.

He stretched his arms toward the ceiling and yawned, the memory of yesterday returning with warmth. Today was his final day on land and he had made plans to spend the day in town with Elsea. The thought brought a smile to his face. Walking, talking, and discovering new places in the passing hours ahead. Almost immediately, the sweetness of it was edged with something jovial and innocent. At sunrise, the ship would leave. And with it, whatever this fragile beginning might become.

He and Elsea had set a meeting spot at the courtyard near the bench by the large tree at ten in the morning. It was now half past 8, and he knew he had to wash up and prepare for the festivities of the day, as well as pack up his belongings for tomorrow morning. However, the thought of what was in store had temporarily stolen his attention.

He wanted today to be special, and his mind was set on making sure he and Elsea would enjoy a pleasant afternoon together. A stroll into town made sense, paying a visit to the new corner bookstore she had mentioned. They were both eager to see what was on the shelves and Homer was hopeful to find answers to his questions.

His mind eased almost immediately as he remembered how natural the conversation flowed with Elsea. Two new friends, drawn together by a shared interest in the bond between animals and people, especially whales. It pained Homer to think about the gory details of those whale hunts his father had forced him to be a part of. Although he had shared a lot already with Elsea, he kept some of the graphics out of their conversation because of the tremendous guilt and shame he felt for taking part in the killing of such beautiful creatures. He knew his time was limited while on land so being intentional with the time spent was all he hoped for.

Homer rose from the bed and began laying out his clothes and supplies to be packed away for tomorrow's departure, moving with an unhurried care he had not felt in days. His journal caught his eye, and he paused to thumb through its worn pages, each entry a quiet record of the dreams that had once weighed so heavily on his waking hours. For weeks, those visions had lingered like fog, pulling at his thoughts and leaving him distracted. This morning brought a rare sense of clarity. The rest he had found in sleep felt earned, almost protective. He decided he would arrive at the courtyard early and bring the journal with him, hoping the stillness before Elsea's arrival might stir a memory or insight worth unfolding. He wanted to be ready to write something the sea had whispered but not yet fully revealed.

Homer inhaled the crisp morning air as he closed the door to his loft. The sunlight brought with it a renewed sense of optimism.

Robert crossed his mind briefly as he hadn't realized how much he missed him and their conversations. Robert was the closest person to him since he left home, and he very much enjoyed his company. Homer was excited to hear all about Robert's hometown adventures, as well as how his girlfriend dynamic had materialized within both families. He was hoping and praying for the best for his friend because he knew how heavily that had been weighing on Robert's mind lately and the anxiety he felt in anticipation of seeing them all for the first time in a while.

Mostly, though, Homer found his thoughts returning to Elsea.

It surprised him how quickly she had taken root in his mind, how easily her presence lingered even when she wasn't speaking. What was unfolding between them felt like a friendship, yes, but one still finding its shape, especially between a young man and a young woman. It was unconventional, perhaps even improper by some standards. Elsea carried herself with a confidence that suggested an old soul, and there was a rebellious edge to her nature that might have been labeled "unladylike" in more rigid circles. Yet that same spirit served her well behind the tavern counter and among the seafaring men who passed through town. She navigated both worlds with ease. In her, Homer sensed a paradox: a student of books and hard-earned experience alike, thoughtful and principled, elegant without pretense, bold without apology.

As they walked, she spoke freely about the town, gesturing toward buildings and alleyways as if each held a story worth telling.

"I grew up knowing which streets to avoid and which ones hide the best surprises," she said with a grin.

Homer smiled. "You make it sound like a map with secret passages."

"Every town has them," she replied. "You just have to be willing to wander."

Something about her words stirred a familiar ache.

In quiet moments, she reminded him of Noko and the way she had always looked beyond the edges of the village, seeing life not as it was confined, but as it could be. His connection to Noko ran deep, shaped by years of shared childhood wonder and unspoken understanding. Homer's longing for her presence had softened in Elsea's company. It did not feel like a betrayal. Rather, it felt like a continuing evolution of a familiar bond that had taught him how to see and listen more deeply. The similarities between Noko and Elsea did not unsettle him. They comforted him, as if some thread in his life had never truly broken, only changed hands.

He had drifted into these thoughts so completely that Elsea's voice startled him.

"Good morning, Homer."

He turned, momentarily disoriented, then smiled as recognition settled in. Her voice was soft, raspy at the edges, almost whisper-like. She stood before him in a long powder-blue dress, a ruffled white blouse peeking out beneath a cropped, wool-trimmed jacket. It was a far cry from her barmaid attire, and for a fleeting moment he felt underdressed by comparison. But the ease between them dissolved the thought just as quickly.

"You look like you were somewhere far away," she teased.

"Maybe I was," he replied. "I didn't mean to miss the time."

"That's alright," she said. "Some places are worth getting lost in."

They fell into easy conversation as she led the way, pointing out familiar corners and quiet shortcuts. Newburyport was changing, she explained, and so were its customs. A young man and woman spending the day together no longer raised many eyebrows, though it might have only a decade earlier. Most gossip, she explained, seemed far more interested in the melodrama unfolding in Vanity Fair than in who was walking with whom.

Their steps carried them toward the district locals referred to as Uptown, a loose gathering of shops arranged in slightly crooked rows. Candle makers worked near hardware stalls. Fishermen's supplies stood beside woodworking shops and apothecaries, barber poles spinning lazily in the morning light. The smell of salt and fresh cut wood lingered in the air. Then, just beyond a fishmonger's stall, the bookstore appeared.

Elsea stopped short. "There it is."

Inside, the shop was long and narrow, its walls lined with shelves that formed a quiet corridor stretching deep into the room. Hundreds of volumes filled the space, their spines creating a muted pattern of color and age.

"I could spend an entire day here," Elsea said, nearly in a whisper.

Homer nodded. "I think I already might."

They had only begun to wander when an elderly, white-haired gentleman approached them.

"Welcome," he said warmly.

"Is there a particular subject you're looking for?"

Homer glanced at Elsea, then back to the man. "Do you have any books on whales," he asked, "and possibly dreams?" The man paused, thinking. "Psychology's two rows over. Medical texts just across from that. And we've a small but growing selection on marine life."

They gathered several books and settled onto a small bench near the back of the store. The shop was quiet, barely open for the day, and the proprietor busied himself nearby, unpacking chests filled with books and setting them carefully onto waiting shelves.

"Last time we spoke," Elsea said gently, "you mentioned a dream. About a whale."

"Indeed," Homer replied. "She's familiar and I recognize she is the eldest of her pod. She doesn't speak, not with words, but it feels as though she's asking something of me."

"What do you think she needs?" Elsea asked.

"I'm not sure," he admitted. "But I sense worry. Fear. As if something tragic has happened or is about to."

She studied him for a moment. "Do you think it's tied to your time hunting with your father?"

"I do," he said quietly. "There's disappointment in her eyes. Expectation. It reaches straight through me."

Elsea grew thoughtful, her fingers resting on the edge of a book as if grounding herself. They spoke for nearly an hour after that about their childhoods, families, friendships, and the fragile balance between livelihood and conscience. Elsea shared all she knew of whales, their intelligence, their vulnerability. She confessed how often she had to bite her tongue at the tavern when whalers spoke too casually of their kills, reminded by her mother that ideals, however noble, could not interfere with survival.

"Ah, here we are," the storekeeper suddenly exclaimed. "I knew I'd find them."

Both Homer and Elsea startled, laughing softly as the man approached with a small stack of books.

"Thank you kindly," Elsea said.

"Yes, thank you, sir," Homer added, feeling lighter than he had in some time. He had shared more of himself than he ever intended and found no judgment waiting for him, only understanding.

As Elsea returned the other books, Homer remained seated, turning his attention to the whale volumes at last. There were three. He ran his fingers along their covers, then paused.

"This," he said, lifting one carefully, "will be the first book I've ever bought."

It was a thick, beautifully bound novel titled Moby-Dick.

Elsea smiled and traced the gilt lettering with her fingertip. Neither spoke for a long moment. The book seemed to hum quietly between them, as if it had joined the conversation in its own way. Homer could not have explained why, but he felt it clearly that something had been set in motion, something that would carry him far beyond this moment, beyond the safety of land and into waters he had not yet learned to navigate.

And though he did not know it then, the calm he felt would not last. The sea would reclaim him, as she always did, patient and indifferent to beginnings.

Chapter Twenty-Two

"Underway, Return to Sea"

Ten months passed in the blink of an eye, and being out at sea had become the norm for Homer, Robert, and the crew of the Pawnee. What once felt unfamiliar had long since become routine. Life underway was no longer something Homer endured. It was a lifestyle he inhabited. The ship, the watch schedules, the constant hum of machinery beneath his feet had become part of his sense of normalcy.

While underway, their responsibilities had shifted in ways that marked time more clearly than any calendar. Homer had earned the title of Boatman's Mate, a quiet promotion that carried weight in expectation rather than ceremony. He now supervised a crew of three men, each responsible for the unglamorous disciplines that kept the ship orderly and alive. Loose equipment had to be secured before seas could turn it into danger. Decks required constant attention, scraped, washed, cleared, then inspected again. During the long night hours, lookout duty demanded patience and vigilance, eyes trained on darkness that could hide anything from floating debris to distant lights on the horizon. Homer learned quickly that leadership was not volume or command, but consistency. Showing up early. Knowing each man's habits. Correcting without humiliating. Holding standards even when fatigue made compromise tempting.

He took the role seriously, not out of ambition, but from a growing respect for the chain that held the ship together. Lives depended on small things done correctly, and he found an unexpected satisfaction in being someone others relied upon. When the work eased and the deck grew quiet, Homer often leaned back against the rail and lifted his eyes toward the night sky. Stars spilled across the darkness in impossible numbers, unbroken by land or city glow, ancient and indifferent. He wondered where this naval life might carry him, what shape his future might take if he continued forward along this course. The world around him felt vast in a way that no longer overwhelmed him. The sky stretched without limit. The sea breathed beneath him, steady and familiar. Even the unknown no longer felt like a threat.

Though he sensed a purpose drawing him onward, it remained indistinct, more pressure than direction. Still, the sea no longer felt like something to survive or escape. What had once come and gone now held, quiet and durable. It felt like a place he belonged. He moved through his days with greater awareness, less resistance, meeting each watch, each task, each sunrise as it arrived, no longer bracing for what the water might take from him.

Robert's days unfolded on a different clock altogether. Training as an engineer kept Robert rotating between the boiler room and control spaces, his shifts opposite Homer's. Their time together had dwindled to brief exchanges or quick conversations snatched between watches, tired laughter in passing corridors. It made them eager for ports, for moments of shared ease where they could sit, talk, and reclaim the rhythm of their friendship. Absence, Homer had learned, sharpened appreciation.

Though Homer had assimilated quite nicely in his new supervisory role in the chain of command, he struggled with the inverted sleep schedule. Fatigue often crept in mid-shift, dulling his focus. He countered it with push-ups on deck, deep breaths of cold night air, anything to stay sharp. He told himself the exhaustion was natural but he knew the truth lay deeper. His dreams were growing heavier, more insistent.

When he did have some down time, he would write letters to Noko and Elsea in his diary, all while knowing he would never share these entries with either of them. Writing became his release, a quiet confession to the page. He carried both women with him, each anchoring him differently. During rare moments of rest, a sense of gratitude and comfort softened his fatigue as he reflected upon his friendships. He missed them deeply, hopeful that fate might one day cross their paths again.

Moby-Dick rarely left his side.

Homer became enthralled as the novel stirred something within. As the story unfolded, it offered him great entertainment while stoking his already active imagination. Homer found echoes of his own life reflected back, looking for connections with the characters, men bound to the sea, consumed by purpose, and people in his own life. Reading it while serving aboard a naval vessel felt uncanny, as though past and present were conversing across the pages. The themes of obsession, reverence, and destruction resonated deeply. The common theme of whales and whale hunting did not go unnoticed by him, either, and it was one of the reasons he chose the book in the first place. He suspected the book had chosen him as much as he had chosen it.

Lately, another presence had begun to intrude upon his waking thoughts: His mother.

Elizabeth began to appear in his dreams now, especially one that lingered with disturbing clarity. In it, she knelt beside a large female whale, Una, lying injured on the shore, her body bloodied. The image perplexed Homer. He could not tell whether the dream was asking something of him or warning him of something already in motion. In it, he struggled to swim ashore, but the current held him fast. His voice failed as he tried to call out to her, sound swallowed before it could reach land. The helplessness clung to him after waking, stirring worry for her well-being and awakening a deep, unshakable homesickness.

Homer had always shared a special bond with his mother. They mirrored one another in quiet sensitivity, carrying compassion beneath composed exteriors. It was his mom who offered him the nurturing and balance in his life, while doing her best to protect him from the volatility of his father. She had been his refuge. Yet, she never stripped Captain Marcus of dignity in Homer's eyes and often reminded him of the shared traits like tenacity, strong will, and a dogged determination to protect and provide for the family. If his father was the storm, Elizabeth was the calm that made endurance possible.

As his awareness began shifting to the present, Homer noticed his time on watch was coming to an end. He stood alongside the rails and took a deep breath, taking in the endless horizon where the night sky met the darkness of the sea. He reflected on how far he had come since joining the Navy. Adolescence had fallen away, replaced by confidence and conviction earned through repetition and responsibility. He no longer shrank from his beliefs, especially his opposition to whale hunting. He did not yet know how he would protect what he loved, only that silence would never again be his bed of refuge.

The rising sun marked the end of his watch, and like curtains closing on the stage of his thinking mind, closing the reflection as he processed all of these thoughts.

He led his crew through final inspections and dismissed them early. Entering the narrow bunk quarters he shared with Robert, he heard whistling.

"You're in a chipper mood," Homer said.

Robert grinned, tightening his boots. "I've decided something."

"Oh?" Homer replied.

Robert exclaimed, "I'm proposing to my girl next time I see her."

Homer blinked. "That's big news. Congratulations!"

Robert clasped his hand firmly. "That's not all. I want you as my best man."

Homer laughed in disbelief. "Me?"

Robert followed, "Wouldn't have it any other way."

"Well then," Homer said softly, emotion catching in his chest, "I'd be honored."

"We'll celebrate at the next port," Robert said. He clapped Homer's shoulder. "Get some rest."

"You too," Homer replied, watching his friend disappear down the corridor, still whistling.

Sleep came quickly, and within minutes the world receded into silence until only Homer's heartbeat remained, steady and hollow, echoing in the dark. From that rhythm, a distant illumination began to form. Light emerged, warped and trembling, and he wondered, Am I dreaming?

At first, the vision appeared as though seen through a veil of water, distorted and wavering, like the world viewed from beneath a waterfall. Then, without warning, he passed through it, as if stepping through parted curtains onto a vast, waiting stage.

His perspective shifted upward, distant, as though seated high in the mezzanine of a grand theatre. Below him stretched a long corridor, pale and endless. Toddler after toddler was guided along its length, their small feet padding softly against the floor. They did not cry. They did not resist. Each was escorted by two tall, faceless sentient beings whose forms seemed unfinished, their outlines flickering as if stitched together from shadow and intention rather than flesh.

At the corridor's end stood a cavernous chamber lined with sealed doors, dozens of them, each engraved with strange markings of gold, as if noting order and identity. One by one, the children were directed toward different thresholds.

Where are they going? Homer wondered, dread tightening in his chest.

The children had come from warmth and safety into this cold, cavernous place, yet they carried something with them, something precious. As Homer focused, his breath caught. Within each child's small body, a soft glow pulsed. Their bellies shimmered faintly, as though filled with liquid gold, radiant and alive.

Why do they have gold inside them? he asked himself. Who put it there and why?

As each door opened, the light from within spilled out, briefly revealing what waited beyond. The air thickened. Shapes moved, low, crouched forms with jagged silhouettes and hollow, waiting eyes. Their presence pressed against the chamber like a sickness, ancient and ravenous. These were not men, yet they carried the intention of men at their worst.

The doors closed quickly, but not before understanding struck him.

The gold was being taken.

He could not see the act itself, yet he felt the moment innocence was claimed, stripped, reduced to fuel. The glow within the children dimmed as the doors shut, swallowed by darkness and firelight beyond. What remained drifted upward as smoke, ash, and silence.

"They are innocent," Homer thought, his heart pounding. Who would do such a thing?

The realization struck him with unbearable force. This was not chaos so much as it resembled industry. A system. A harvest.

The chamber filled with soundless screams that vibrated through his bones. His heartbeat thundered like a ticking bomb. He tried to cry out, but his voice was gone. He tried to run, but his body would not obey. He was trapped in what seemed an unwilling witness to a ritual of consumption where purity was currency and life was reduced to resource.

The abyss beyond the doors teemed with hungry fanged shadows driven appetite rather than rage. A calculated, endless appetite for what was pure.

Sharp grief tore through Homer's chest as the final door closed. He understood now that the vision spoke to what the world does to innocence, how it extracts value, burns what remains, and calls it progress.

The image seared itself into him. This was not a dream meant to fade.

Chapter Twenty-Three

"Explosion"

The ship screamed before it shook. The explosion tore Homer from sleep like a cannon fired inside his skull.

A violent shockwave reverberated through the berthing space, his body lifted, then slammed back down as loose gear crashed to the floor. The force jolted Homer upright, heart hammering. It was as though the ocean itself had risen and struck the hull with a clenched fist.

It was a dream. A damn dream. "Thank God," he muttered, dragging in a breath thick with relief.

Ten seconds passed as if time had slowed down.

Then another in what felt like an eternity.

But the relief curdled in an instant.

A deep, metallic groan reverberated through the hull of the Pawnee followed by alarms of crew members screaming in layered chaos. Boots thundered overhead with the muffled sound of men shouting. Somewhere below deck, something burned with a roar that sounded alive.

In a flash, Homer realized this was not a dream.

He swung his legs over the bunk and burst into the corridor just as a wave of heat rushed up the passageway. Smoke crawled along the ceiling like a living thing.

"What the hell was that?" he shouted.

No one answered him directly, only the stampede of sailors rushing past, faces pale, eyes wide. He fell in with them, running blind until a familiar voice finally cut through the din.

"There's been an explosion in the boiler room!" the quartermaster yelled. "God help them, it's bad!"

The words struck Homer like a blade.

He immediately thought of Robert.

In a moment without careful reasoning, Homer deliberately broke from the group and sprinted toward the engine room. Suddenly, he was seized upon by a strong arm, catching him across the chest, and slammed him back against the bulkhead.

"Hold fast!" barked Captain Adams, appearing through the smoke like a man carved from iron. "No one goes below without orders!"

Homer looked up at him, wild-eyed. "Sir, Brown is down there with the engine crew."

Captain Adams didn't soften, but his jaw tightened. "I know. And if you rush in now, you'll only add another body to the count."

He turned sharply. "Fire parties! Buckets, pumps, and hoses, move! I want a line formed from the deck to the boiler access, now!

You," he pointed at Homer, "you look able. Get those men organized."

Adrenaline drowned grief.

"Yes, sir."

Homer moved like instinct given flesh, in a subtle way he resembled Marcus with directing hands, snapping orders, hauling pumps into place. Buckets filled and passed, metal clanging, water sloshing as smoke thickened and heat pressed closer. Somewhere beneath them, fire roared as if fed by rage itself.

"Connect the pump!" Adams shouted. "Keep the line tight! Don't break formation!"

As Homer worked, his eyes kept drifting to the scorched corridor leading down. The boiler-room hatch was blackened, warped outward like a wound torn open. Steam hissed from within, carrying the unmistakable stench of burnt oil and flesh.

His heart sank.

Then he heard what sounded like a low, concussive whoomp as something inside collapsed.

That was all it took for Homer to break.

He shoved past the line. "Robert!" he yelled, already running.

"Homer, no!" someone shouted behind him.

As he passed the threshold, the heat hit him like a wall. Steam blasted from ruptured pipes, scalding his legs as he pressed deeper into the smoke filled chamber. A fragment of iron, likely boiler shrapnel, sheared loose from above and tore into his right thigh, another slashing across his lower abdomen as he stumbled forward.

Pain exploded in his body but out of sheer adrenaline, he kept moving.

The boiler door had blown completely off its hinges, the furnace inside glowing like a gaping mouth from hell. The cause was already clear to trained eyes: pressure trapped behind a failed valve, heat building unchecked until the furnace door finally surrendered in a violent release. The engine room was devastated with twisted metal, collapsed beams, bodies thrown like broken dolls.

"Homer! Get out of there!" someone screamed. But he didn't hear them.

He searched through smoke and flame, choking on ash, calling Robert's name until his voice broke. But there was no answer. Only silence and the still truth carried on the air. Nothing alive remained.

His strength failed until he began to collapse.

The last thing he felt was hands grabbing him and pulling him to safety as the world tilted sideways. Soaked blankets smothered his burning clothes as men dragged him back through the inferno. Captain Adams himself dropped to his knees beside Homer, barking orders while pressing his hands to Homer's chest, forcing breath back into him.

"Breathe, son! Stay with me!"

Light flickered at the edges of Homer's vision as pain bloomed everywhere at once: his leg, his ribs, his gut. This isn't a dream, he realized dimly. This is the price.

When consciousness returned fully, the fire was out.

Robert and the other engineers in the boiler room were gone.

"Easy now, Homer," a voice said gently.

He turned his head, or rather tried to, aware of the pain limiting his range of motion. The movement sent knives through his side.

"Where's Robert?" he whispered.

The Master at Arms, Nathaniel Goodman, stood beside the ship's doctor and loblolly boy. The faces all shared a grave burden with the sense of loss. "Deep… there was nothing anyone could have done. He died instantly. All three of them did."

"No," Homer croaked. "No!"

Tears came hard and fast, dragging sobs from somewhere deep and broken. Pain surged up his right side as if echoing the loss itself. This was the first time Homer had experienced loss of this magnitude in his life. It felt close and personal.

"You ran into fire for another man," Goodman said quietly. "That's not something this ship will forget."

"But it didn't save him," Homer whispered.

"No," the man replied softly. "But it says everything about who you are."

As morphine dulled the edges of the world, Homer's eyes glazed over. The last thing he said before darkness took him was a single name, spoken like a prayer and a wound all at once.

"Robert."

Chapter Twenty-Four

"Stranded"

The name lingered long after his lips went numb.

Morphine pulled Homer downward in slow, uneven waves. He did not fall into sleep, nor into dreams, but into something hollow and suspended, a place without edges or direction. Time fractured. Voices drifted in and out as some seemed close, some more distant, but they never stayed long enough to be understood. Faces hovered above him, blurred and distorted, then vanished as if erased by water. Somewhere beyond the fog, the ship creaked and groaned like a wounded animal refusing to die, its strained timbers complaining with every subtle roll of the sea.

Hours later, when Homer regained consciousness, the pain was still there. A deep, throbbing ache radiated through his leg and lower abdomen, flaring sharply whenever he shifted. His mouth was dry, his tongue thick, and his throat burned as if he had swallowed sand. The air smelled of salt, oil, and smoke that had long since cooled. The sea was still there. The ship was still afloat.

But Robert was gone.

His absence settled over Homer with a sharp finality. There was no way to protest or rewind the clock which would usher Robert's return. It pressed into his chest and hollowed him out, leaving him numb in ways the morphine never could.

Between the sporadic updates from the doctor's loblolly boy, the hushed exchanges of shipmates, and the constant shuffle of boots and rigging, Homer came to understand what no one said outright: the crew was at the mercy of Mother Nature now. And to make matters more challenging, the wind shifted into absence as if Robert had carried it away with him to yonder places. The ocean currents dominated every conversation as well, with every worried glance toward the horizon. For the better part of a week, Homer lay in his bunk listening, watching shadows move across the bulkheads, waiting for news that never brought relief.

Twenty-seven men had been adrift for eleven days.

The explosion had crippled the ship's steam power beyond repair. The engine room that was once the beating heart of the vessel was now a blackened ruin sealed off like a tomb. With no steam, progress toward land was painfully slow. The paddle wheel offered limited maneuverability, but it demanded relentless manual labor. Men rotated through exhausting shifts, their bodies already weakened by hunger and thirst. Rations had been strictly enforced, and it showed. Faces grew gaunt. Tempers shortened. Movements slowed. Restlessness had given way to lethargy, and lethargy was slowly fermenting into fear.

Fresh water was the most immediate concern. The irony was merciless, surrounded by an endless expanse of water that could not save them. The sea shimmered and slapped against the hull as if mocking their thirst, reminding all twenty-seven men of its indifference.

To preserve order and sanity, the ship's leaders gathered the crew twice daily. Duties were assigned. Information was shared, however limited. The ship's two first mates worked tirelessly over navigation charts, recalculating and recalculating again, searching for a margin of hope. Goodman's voice remained steady, despite the strain in his eyes, and maintained order with the crew wherever possible.

"We'll need food," he said during one such gathering. "Every bit we can manage. Ideas?"

From desperation came ingenuity. Leftover bacon grease from the galley was smeared onto crudely fashioned hooks. Lines were tied to makeshift poles assembled from spare wood and cordage. Fishing became both a necessity as well as providing a distraction for the crew, something else to focus on besides thirst and uncertainty. The men worked together, calling out to one another as they hauled lines and adjusted their grip. Short instructions, encouragement, and the occasional joke passed between them, filling the air with sound and purpose. In that shared effort, isolation loosened its hold, replaced by the steady reassurance of voices and bodies moving toward the same end.

In three days, they caught one fish.

It was scarcely enough to divide in any meaningful way, thin portions passed from hand to hand, more symbolic than sustaining, but it lifted spirits all the same. The smell of cooked fish drifted briefly through the galley, and for a moment it felt like abundance. Men chewed slowly, savoring each bite, eyes closed as if memory itself might fill the emptiness in their bellies. For a few precious hours, hope flickered, not boldly, but enough to warm the edges of despair.

Desperation, however, has a way of bending into absurdity. At one point, a gull swooped low over the rail, bold or foolish enough to linger, and the deck erupted into sudden movement. A sailor lunged, fingers brushing feathers, the promise of a meal nearly within reach. All of the sudden, the bird burst free in a frantic explosion of feathers, shrieking indignantly as it vanished into the sky. The crew froze for a heartbeat, then groaned in unison, equal parts disappointment and disbelief.

That night, as darkness settled and lanterns burned low, the story grew with each retelling. The gull became larger, the reach closer, the escape more dramatic. Laughter, thin and tired but real, rippled across the ship, breaking the long silence that hunger and fear had imposed. It was a fragile sound, easily lost to the sea, but for that moment it reminded them of something essential. They were still men. Capable of humor. Still alive.

Despite everything, the crew tried to remain optimistic. But even the stoic composure of the officers began to crack. Conversations dropped into whispers. Concern crept into voices meant to reassure. Homer noticed it in the pauses, in the way men stared longer at the horizon than necessary.

As his body slowly healed, Homer decided the infirmary was not where he wished to spend his final days, that is if his final days were indeed approaching. There was little resistance from the doctor or his loblolly boy when Homer requested to return to his bunk. Pain now served as a distraction, dulling the sharper edges of grief. Yet sleeping in the quarters he had once shared with Robert reopened wounds no bandage could cover.

Hunger gnawed constantly. His stomach cramped and growled, competing with the stinging pain of healing burns and scabbed skin. The morphine supply dwindled quickly, until there was none left at all.

It was then he remembered a conversation with his father.

Captain Marcus had once told him stories of his first whale hunt and of how hunger so severe it stripped away hesitation and left only necessity. “Do you know what it’s like to go hungry?” his father had asked, not unkindly. At the time, Homer had not understood as deeply. Now, lying adrift in the middle of an endless ocean with nothing to drink, the words carried a brutal clarity.

For the first time, Homer felt empathy for the father he had long resented. He saw the animal world differently now, not as something to conquer or exploit, but as something intrinsically entangled with survival. Mother Nature was no longer romantic. She was sovereign.

The rhythmic clapping of water against the hull was once soothing but now became a constant reminder of their paralysis. The wind had abandoned them entirely. Sails hung limp and useless. Under ideal conditions, land was four or five days away. These were far from ideal.

With only two flares remaining, the decision was made to fire one the following day, a desperate gamble that someone, anyone, might see it.

That evening, the crew gathered amid coils of rope and dim lantern light, passing the last jug of rum hand to hand. No one spoke at first. The liquid burned going down with a sharp unforgiving tinge but it warmed places the cold had begun to claim.

“To Robert, fair winds and following seas!” the Captain finally said, lifting the jug slightly.

“To Robert,” several voices echoed, uneven but sincere.

A younger sailor wiped his mouth with the back of his hand. “Man could fix an engine with half the tools missing,” he said quietly.

"Did it once in port, swore he didn't need the rest."

A low chuckle passed through the group.

"Aye," another added. "And cursed the whole time like the boiler had wronged him personally."

Someone laughed too loudly. Someone else sniffed and looked away.

"He sang, too," a deckhand said after a pause. "When he thought no one could hear. Always off-key."

"That's because you lot don't know music," came a reply. "Robert did."

The jug made another slow circuit. Voices loosened with the rum.

A man near the rail began to hum, tentative at first, then steadier. Others joined in, some remembering the tune, others inventing their way through it. The song was old, older than any of them, a sailor's lament about home, loss, and the sea's indifference. The words blurred and overlapped, but the meaning held.

Leave her Johnny, leave her…

Homer sat apart, the sound washing over him. For a moment, he could almost see Robert there with his elbows on knees, head tipped back, singing louder than necessary.

The song ended without ceremony.

"Fair winds and following seas," the Captain said again, softer this time.

"Aye," Goodman answered. "Wherever he's headed."

The jug ran dry.

Homer recognized the phrase from hushed conversations between his father and uncles, a phrase spoken only when a sailor man had fallen. The ritual was beautiful. And unbearable.

As the crew drifted into a quiet, rum-soaked slumber, Homer already knew what he intended to do.

He tried to slow his thoughts, to imagine a way to still be useful, something other than a burden, a liability. But nothing came. Only the desire to escape the pain and the suffocating sense of doom. It struck him then, distantly, that his mind had not reached for those he loved. Their names hovered at the edge of awareness like stars behind heavy cloud cover, ever present but unreachable. It was not that he loved them less, but that the weight of loving them felt unbearable in this moment. To think of them would mean imagining their faces upon discovering his failure, their grief becoming another thing he would have caused, another debt he could not repay.

Restless, he rose and searched for something, anything, that could help him walk. A cane. A crutch. He moved through the empty mess hall into the kitchen, dragging his body along bulkheads for support. After pushing aside loose metal, he found table legs stored beneath shelving. One was nearly the right size.

For thirty minutes, he worked painstakingly, repositioning it again and again. When it was finally right, he pressed down and snapped it free. The makeshift cane wasn't perfect, but it helped.

Exhaustion overtook him soon after and he laid on the deck, closing his eyes for what he thought would be a minute. The effects of the rum are still slightly hanging on.

A short time later, he woke in a cold sweat.

Faces filled his mind of his mother Elizabeth, his siblings, his father. What are they going to think? He thought to himself. Noko appeared next, her reverence for life burning painfully bright in contrast to his thoughts. Childhood friends followed. Then Elsea, and the regret of never reconnecting with those he loved and cared for.

He clutched his diary in the darkness, grateful he could not see the page. No words would make sense. Some things were better left unwritten.

His decision was made. In this narrowed state, his thoughts obeyed a cruel economy: only what hurt directly was allowed to remain. Memory collapsed inward. Hope felt irresponsible. Love felt like another obligation he could no longer meet. Even Noko, whose presence once steadied him, now felt too vast to hold. To reach for her would require faith, a faith that he was still worth anchoring, that his existence had not already tipped into liability. He reasoned his absence would be better, giving the crew a better chance of survival. And so his mind chose the simpler path, the quieter cruelty of erasure, where escape seemed easier than endurance, and absence felt like the only mercy he could still offer the ones he loved.

Before dawn, before watch began, Homer made his way to the ship's stern. Several agonizing minutes passed before he reached the edge. The stars shone above him, indifferent. There was still a choice. But his mind no longer recognized it. Perhaps his demise would be retold as an unfortunate accident. Whatever the outcome, he intended on not being alive to see it.

Without hesitation, he tipped forward and fell overboard.

The sea swallowed him with a moderate splash.

No human eyes saw the act. But fourteen others watched closely.

As water closed over him, instinct surged. He fought, panicked, questioned everything. Guilt burned. Would Robert's death be in vain if I die? He thought. The thought splintered, chased by a dozen others, each one sharp, each one demanding an answer he no longer had. He fought for what felt like forever before exhaustion claimed him. His limbs began cramping and his lungs burned from the salt water that crept inside. In what he thought was a final glance, he saw the Pawnee as she continued drifting further away. Swimming in the cold waters was challenging enough but reaching her, with the distance that had grown between them, was out of the question.

As he began sinking into the abyss, the whales arrived.

Seven of them.

One emerged from the rest and lifted him gently, deliberately, on the bulk of her back. He touched her skin, smooth and cool beneath his hand. Homer sensed there was a timeless connection. In her eyes, he recognized Astra. Together the pod returned him back to the ship.

With a sudden push and an answering pull, grace itself set him upon the deck, soaked to the bone and trembling. Homer broke into tears, undone by exhaustion and awe. A power greater than his own had reached into the depths and drawn him back from himself.

"I'm alive," he whispered with sheer gratitude.

Above him, the stars finally revealed themselves. And within him, he felt the voice of Om with a vibration that was ancient and resonant, speaking to his soul. This time Una was witness to Homer as the words vibrated with energy between them:

You will live. And you will learn to appreciate life in all forms and varieties.

Chapter Twenty-Five

"Rescued"

The deck was still damp beneath his feet, the night air sharp against his skin, when Homer finally trusted his legs enough to move. Each step sent a twinge through his injured leg, but it was a welcoming reminder that he was still here. It took Homer a few agonizing moments to make his way back to his bunk, and not a soul noticed him. Hunger, exhaustion, and rum had claimed the crew. For now, the rescue belonged only to him, the whales, and the sea.

He would have lingered on the deck, letting the sunrise wash over him, but duty of a different sort called. With trembling hands, he removed his soaked clothing, tending to his wounds with the careful motions of habit. Only then did he reach for his diary. The pages seemed to quiver beneath his fingers as he wrote:

"If I had not experienced what had just happened myself, I never would believe such an occurrence could take place. It could read well as a tale, but I know better. This was a gift of divine intervention. I will cherish it, draw upon it for strength, and honor it by preserving my life. I will appreciate each breathing moment as a gentle reminder of the gift life holds, and of the duty that comes with it."

He paused, letting the words settle, then bowed his head. A simple, humble prayer followed with a quiet gratitude and relief for his past failings. He called upon the heavens and sea for protection and safe passage to land for the Pawnee and crew.

A whistling sound drew him from his reverie, rising in the quiet corridor. Homer stiffened before standing upright. Was it a trick of his senses? The sound sharpened, stronger now, a rushing movement that threaded through the ship's compartments. Then a thought struck: "My God, it's the wind!" he blurted out.

Grabbing his makeshift cane, he shuffled from doorway to doorway, clanking the end against the floor and railing. "The wind is blowing! Get up, all hands on deck!" His voice echoed down the corridor, and slowly, like a rising tide, the crew stirred. One by one, the tired, hungover men emerged, blinking and coughing, until the ship's human heartbeat pulsed once more. Before long the Captain's voice rose above the stirrings. "Lift the sails! Catch the wind and drive her forward!" The men surged into motion, hauling ropes, bracing against the swaying deck. Homer steadied himself against a railing, eyes wide, as sails unfurled for the first time in weeks. The creaking of the timbers and flapping of canvas blended into music, an anthem of survival.

The faint sounds of morning grew into the noise of a bustling crew, louder with each gust of wind. Homer breathed in, the noise of the deck filling him, and for the first time since the injury, his body answered without protest. There was a high energy among the crew that coincided with the forward motion of the ship. Homer realized that the sounds he heard were hopeful men working the sails, which had not been in use for weeks. The sight of the upright sails being filled by the steady winds brought a smile to Homer's face, followed by tears. He stood there longer than he meant to.

A crewmate offered his arm. “We’re making headway. If this keeps up, we could be near land in forty-eight hours!” Homer gripped it, leaning heavily, and together they watched the sails billow, catching the morning light. “I’m glad she’s here,” the crewmate said softly, eyes on the horizon. “Mother Nature sure is an unpredictable dame.” Homer smiled through the lingering ache in his body. “She sure is,” Homer said, still watching the sails.

Voices rose from the bow, shouts and laughter carried across the deck. Out of curiosity, he moved closer to see what all the excitement was about. “Look! Half a dozen whales!” someone yelled. His heart lifted as he approached the edge and saw her. It was Astra and her pod, the same creatures who had saved him, now frolicking through the swells. They led the way, guiding the ship, playful and sure. Astra surfaced close enough that he could see the pale scars along her flank before she slipped back beneath the swell. Homer’s breath caught, and for a fleeting moment, he saw Robert there, laughing, alive in memory, riding the waves alongside him.

Homer peered out to the majestic whales and briefly the pangs of hunger were distracted by the beauty that surrounded them. Homer took it all in and reflected upon his journey. The whales had always been in his life in one capacity or another. He felt connected to them in ways he couldn’t articulate before. He knew they were a part of him, and his empathy and admiration for them ran deep within his soul.

Exhaustion became secondary to purpose. Every man worked with a renewed rhythm, eyes darting between the horizon, the sails, and the water’s playful movements. Now that the tides had literally turned, there was an intense desire to make it to port before something else went wrong like fading winds, starvation, or even sinking from a tattered ship. These possibilities surely crossed the minds of the shipmates. The storm clouds that had loomed were replaced with the gleam of dawn and the splendor of wind in the rigging. Fortunately, the winds of change had certainly been in their favor, and the result was a finely-tuned crew of men working in unison for a common cause. Survival, once a struggle, now carried momentum.

Several hours had passed before the skies cracked with thunder and rain poured down on the ship and the men. Buckets were set to catch the precious water; men laughed and shouted in the cleansing downpour. The storm offered more than relief from thirst. It became a baptism for the crew who had endured so much. It also created the perfect tailwind to further advance the ship toward its destination. Tears mixed with rain, each sailor processing the events in his own quiet subtle way. Pain and loss remained, but now hope, faith, and gratitude filled the spaces between. The crew peered out and saw land for the first time in months.

Too exhausted for celebration, relief settled quietly among the men who had somehow defied the odds and reached port. As the ship eased into safety, Homer remained inwardly tethered to the events of the last few days, his thoughts returning again and again to Astra and her pod. Gratitude welled within him. The very beings he had watched suffer at the hands of men were the same ones who had carried him, and the ship to some extent, back from the edge. It felt impossible, yet undeniable. Somewhere beyond reason, a divine power had intervened.

Still, one question echoed in the stillness of his mind.

Why?

As he sat on the deck, memories stirred over his first encounter with whales as a boy, the quiet awe, the sense of recognition he had never been able to name. But what unsettled him most were the visions that followed. He saw himself among them, moving through the water, bearing the same grief. He felt the weight of loss as a whale might, beaching in sorrow, calling out to a presence that would never return. And he felt it as a man. First Kai. Then Robert. The pain was the same, crossing form and flesh, binding him to them in ways he was only beginning to understand.

"Get the ropes!" came the call from a boatswain's mate as land finally rose before them. Within a few hundred yards, the familiar Newburyport harbor waited with unmoving solidarity, alive with onlookers who surged forward, eager to help as the wounded ship crept toward safety. Longshoremen instinctively rushed to their stations.

"Hold her steady!" the captain commanded.

Lines flew outward, coiling through the air before landing in outstretched hands on shore. Slowly and almost reverently, the ship was guided portside, her hull easing into harbor as if she, too, exhaled. Homer felt his knees weaken as relief washed through him. For the first time in months, safety was no longer an idea, but a place beneath his feet.

Hands reached for the crew. Water was passed. Voices offered comfort. What had unfolded at sea could only be called a miracle. As strangers welcomed them like kin, Homer felt the quiet power of humanity revealed in its truest form. How can man be so cruel in one moment and so compassionate in the next? he wondered, holding the question gently, without judgment.

Then, cutting through the noise, a friendly voice called his name.

"Homer! Homer!"

He turned, breath caught in his chest. There, he saw through the crowd, stood Elsea. Her countenance seemed radiant. There she was, so real and alive, his eyes could hardly believe what they saw. The sound of her voice collapsed the distance between past and present, grief and grace. Against all odds, he had returned to the land, and to a loving friendship bringing comfort to his tired soul.

Homer drew in a long, trembling breath as the world settled back into place. Clarity arrived without effort or explanation. The whales, the wind, the wounded ship, the suffering and the salvation no longer felt separate to him. He did not know why he had been spared. Only that he had. And that knowledge carried with it a quiet vow: never again would he treat breath, life, or love as expendable.

Time moved differently after that.

Chapter Twenty-Six

"The Good Doctor"

"Liberty, Liberty, Liberty!" shouted Captain Adams from the quarterdeck.

The urgency that governed every hour at sea loosened its grip, replaced by a gentler awareness of voices, of warmth. The crew was guided from the docks into familiar streets, their injuries tended, their hunger answered. By the time they gathered again beneath the low beams and amber light of the tavern they had once known, the enormity of their survival began to settle in.

Homer felt with tangible certainty he and the crew had been carried to this place and moment by hands far larger than their own. The events of the past forty-eight hours defied doctrine, reason, and belief alike, slipping past the boundaries of any single faith. And yet here they were again, gathered in familiar warmth, welcomed not as strangers but as returned men. They felt safe in the convivial tavern, eating and drinking to their heart's content, after escaping the throes of death by way of hunger or drowning. Measured against logic, it made no sense at all. But within the shared relief and quiet reverence of survival, it felt entirely fitting.

Any attempt to unravel the miraculous nature of the events would have to wait for another day. There would be time later, through ink and reflection, for Homer to attempt to understand what had transpired. For now, the men surrendered themselves fully to the moment: warm plates passed along the tables, mugs raised and emptied, music swelling, bodies moving, stories flowing. In Elsea's small family tavern along the wharf, the truest expression of human community revealed itself with life affirmed, suffering momentarily softened, gratitude given room to breathe.

The gravity of it all was not lost on Homer. In two days' time, he had borne witness to what he could only name as miracles. First, the intervention of Astra and her pod. Then, the wind rose as if summoned, driving their wounded ship safely into harbor. The first would remain his secret. Spoken aloud, it would sound like madness, even to himself. And yet, the memory took root inside him, like lightning frozen in stone. "This memory isn't a dream," Homer thought. "It's here, inside me, in my bones and in my heart. I can feel it, every moment, every pulse." He carried it inside him, undeniable and permanent.

Then there was Elsea.

Her serendipitous presence here, at the same port where their paths had first crossed months earlier, settled into his thoughts like a third, quieter miracle. For a fleeting moment, Homer searched for meaning, for some greater pattern he might name or claim. But the thought dissolved as music swelled and laughter rose around him. The Tavern Inn was alive with voices. The crew shared their story with eager listeners, retelling hardship and near loss with the awe of men who had returned from the edge. To the townspeople, they were heroes. To one another, they were simply alive.

Goodman's hand found Homer's shoulder, firm and grounding. Homer turned and met his grasp, the familiarity of it steadying him. He drew a slow breath before saying quietly, "Thank you, sir. For everything." They held the grip longer than custom required. Finally, Goodman cleared his throat.

"We weren't out there all alone, Deep," he said. "Not for a moment. And the men saw your resolve, your fight. It mattered. I know the loss of Robert cut deep. It cut us all. But I know it cuts you most."

Homer nodded, unable to offer more. The words were enough, a quiet acknowledgment of the gratitude and respect he felt, but they carried more weight than he could express aloud.

A brief shadow of shame passed through him as he replayed the moment he had plunged into the sea, intent on ending his suffering. A moment of despair, he thought. One he would have to forgive. Even now, though the miraculous events that followed had saved his life, Homer knew forgiveness for that desperate choice would be a personal journey. He drew in a slow breath and closed his eyes, recalling the vow he had made on the deck of the Pawnee.

Astra's steady gaze returned to him, and with it, the resolve to live more thankfully, more faithfully, more fully. Those fleeting thoughts of regret began to dissolve like morning mist, leaving room for something stronger. Yes! Homer's life would carry new meaning, a renewed purpose, and a sense of adventure that even fear and despair could not diminish.

He scanned the tavern, letting his gaze settle on familiar faces, familiar sounds, and moments already etched into memory. Elsea moved through the crowd with effortless grace, balancing mugs of ale and plates of steaming food. Homer noticed a customer, a man in a tweed jacket and wool scarf, bowing slightly in conversation.

Their eyes met, and Elsea's glance caught his. Normally, he would have turned away, a pang of self-consciousness holding him back, but not this time. He stood his ground and returned her smile, feeling warmth and recognition blossom in his chest. She lifted a hand and gestured, mouthing the words: "Homer, come over here, please."

Homer meandered carefully through the busy floor, dodging chairs and laughing patrons, until he reached her. She took his hand gently and guided him toward the man. "Homer, I'd like you to meet Dr. Charles Young," she said, her voice carrying a quiet authority that made Homer instantly feel welcomed.

The man rose, extending his hand. "Pleasure to meet you, Sir," Homer said with sincerity.

"Please," Dr. Young interrupted, a kind smile spreading across his face, "call me Charles."

Elsea's eyes twinkled as she added, "He's a specialist in psychology and dreams, Homer. He's here in town on a speaking engagement and heard about your ship's ordeal." She leaned in quickly and whispered to Homer, her tone conspiratorial and cheerful: "He's also the one covering the crew's meal tonight." Before Homer could respond, she excused herself with a light nod and a wink, leaving the two men facing each other.

Homer relaxed into the conversation, drawn in by Charles' calm confidence. "Thank you for your generosity, Charles," he said. "The pleasure is mine. You have no idea what your kindness means to us."

Charles inclined his head, eyes attentive and warm. "You and your crew have endured something extraordinary, Homer. Traumatic and courageous, perhaps even miraculous. Moments like these remind us of the resilience of the human spirit."

Homer's lips curved into a small, genuine smile. "I, I never expected to meet someone so invested in the human mind and the world of dreams. I've had experiences lately… strange dreams, vivid ones, that I can hardly explain."

Charles leaned forward, intrigued. "I would be honored to hear about them, if you wish. Only when you're ready, and only if you want to share. No obligation whatsoever."

Homer hesitated a moment, considering the invitation. Then, with the trust that had been building since the ship's safe harbor, he said, "I'd very much like that."

A smile crossed Charles' face, and he raised his mug. "Very well. For now, let us enjoy the moment. To life, to survival, and to the mysteries that make it all worth living." Homer mirrored the gesture, clinking his mug gently against Charles'. "To life, and the sea," he echoed.

The tavern buzzed around them, filled with laughter, clinking mugs, and the soft strains of music. Homer allowed himself to be present, letting the warmth of companionship and the celebration of survival wash over him. For the first time in a fortnight he felt himself settle back into the world, restored by friendship, warmth, and the steady pulse of life.

Chapter Twenty-Seven

"Midnight Oil"

Hours later, the tavern had quieted. Most of the Navy men had returned to their lodgings, and the clatter from the kitchen had slowed to a gentle rhythm. Homer and Charles remained, talking long into the night, candlelight flickering against their faces. Elsea had long since excused herself, encouraging them to stay as long as they wished and reminding them to blow out the candle before leaving.

Homer leaned back, settling into the worn wooden chair, feeling the fatigue of recent days press against him with a familiar weight. The conversation shifted naturally toward the curious, the uncanny, and the profound. He led the conversation with his dreams, the strange visions that had haunted and guided him since the voyage, and the truths they seemed to whisper.

"Tell me about the lizard and the snake," Charles said, his tone gentle but insistent, leaning forward with the intensity of someone who truly wanted to understand.

Homer exhaled slowly, letting the memory rise into the present. "It was the strangest dream... and yet, somehow, it feels like it was trying to tell me something. Something important." And as the candle burned low, their dialogue deepened, drawing Homer further from the tangible world and closer to what he carried within. He relaxed in the ambiance, staring into his near empty schooner as though the ale might give him courage.

"I wasn't sure at first if I was the lizard or just watching it," he began, voice unsteady. "But there it was, jaws locked around a snake, trying to eat it from the tail. The damn thing kept slipping out, twisting, sliding away. I was getting nowhere, just wearing myself out. Then I felt it. A pressure. I just instantly knew. The words flashed into my mind.

"Go for the head. Crush it first."

He clenched his fists at the memory. "So I did. I went to the head, sunk my teeth in, and felt the skull break between my jaws. Then I swallowed it whole. One gulp. It was brutal, but it worked. And afterward it was… quiet. Almost easy." Homer exhaled, shaking his head.

"I keep wondering what the hell it meant. Maybe the lizard was me. Maybe the snake was… something else. A demon? A woman, maybe? Or a force in the world that waits patiently for its chance. You know the kind… something that coils around you slowly, tightening until you can't breathe, and then swallows you whole. Crafty, smiling as it takes everything. Like some old fable or a serpent in the garden. Maybe it was a warning, a reminder of the dangers out there that every young man should be wary of before the world claims him."

The words hung heavy between them. Homer looked up, half-expecting Charles to flinch, but the older man's face stayed calm, even kind.

Charles folded his hands, his voice low and steady. “Interesting. Snakes and lizards… ancient symbols. They’ve haunted dreams and myths since the first stories were told. To some, they are evil. To others, they can represent wisdom. Perhaps they are both. You may see the snake as a woman or demon, but often it is something deeper like your own shadow. The part of you that fears being consumed, overpowered, lost.”

He leaned forward slightly, closing the gap between them. “And the voice that told you to strike at the head? That may have been your deeper self. A reminder that fear is never defeated from the sideline, it must be faced strategically. Only then can it be swallowed and made part of you.”

Homer’s brow furrowed, his breath slowing as he considered this. He took the last gulp of his ale, while the momentum of releasing what he had held inside for so long, had him opening up much more than he expected. Before tonight, Noko, Elsea, and his diary were the only ones with whom he confided and shared his dreams. Never before would he feel comfortable to talk about such things especially with another man.

Charles was different. He was a stranger and a friend at the same time, much like a mate who has a conversation in a pub after a few pints, as stories and tales are unloaded comfortably without any guilt or need to show proof. However, the dialogue between Charles and Homer had a quality to it like that of an uncle to a nephew, or a chat with a lifelong friend. There was an added weight to his words, shaped by years as a physician and student of the mind, someone who had devoted his life to understanding the inner lives of others.

Charles leaned back slightly, cradling his schooner between both hands, the candlelight catching in the fine lines around his eyes. There was no urgency in him, no hunger to impress, only a patient attentiveness as though time itself had agreed to slow in his presence.

"As Elsea may have mentioned," he said gently, "I've devoted much of my life to the study of dreams and how the mind speaks when the body finally loosens its grip on the world." He smiled faintly, almost apologetically. "Some men spend their years charting stars to move across the seas. I chose the inner sky and oceans of the mind."

Homer listened, drawn in by the calm certainty in Charles's voice.

"In all my years of study," Charles continued, "across universities, clinics, and places far less refined than either, I have come to accept something that once unsettled me greatly." He paused, letting the tavern's distant sounds fill the space between them. "There are regions of the psyche that do not yield to measurement. No equation, no chemical formula, no anatomical chart can fully account for them. And yet," he said softly, "they govern us all the same."

He lifted his schooner, took a slow sip, then set it down carefully.

"Dreams do not always speak plainly," he went on. "They borrow costumes. They shape themselves from symbol and sensation. Snakes, lizards, and demons. They appear often in the dreams of thoughtful men." A small, reassuring smile crossed his face. "But they are rarely what they seem, appearing as fragments of ourselves we have not yet learned how to carry."

Homer shifted slightly in his seat.

"They wear many masks," Charles said. "Sometimes the face of a stranger. Sometimes the face of someone we love. Sometimes... our own." His gaze softened. "The dream is not asking to be feared, Homer. It reveals what waking life has forced into shadow. It is asking to be understood."

He leaned forward then, as a fellow traveler. He studied Homer carefully, as one might study a landscape before crossing it.

"Tell me," Charles asked quietly, "what is your relationship like with your mother?"

The question lingered between them, deliberate and unhurried. It carried the weight of intention, opening a quiet space where something honest might emerge.

Homer lowered his gaze, his voice softening. "My mother... She is the gentlest soul I have ever known. Where my father's words were commands, hers were comfort. She carried a patience that could calm any storm. When I was a young child, it was her arms that shielded me from his temper, her voice that reminded me there was kindness in the world. I suppose whatever compassion I have comes from her."

He paused, a faint smile painted across his lips. "I remember one night, there had been a storm at sea, and the house shook with the wind. My father barked orders even at home, telling us to be still, to endure it like men. But I was just a boy, terrified. My mother found me trembling under the table. She wrapped her shawl around me, pulled me to her chest, and whispered that the storm would pass, that no darkness lasted forever. She rocked me like I was still a baby, and for the first time I believed it. I clung to her, not the pillows and blankets in the makeshift bunker under the dining table, and somehow I felt safe."

The smile faded, leaving only a quiet ache in his tone. "She never spoke against him. Not directly. But I could see it in the light of her eyes that she wished for me a life different from the one he demanded. A life not bound by harpoons and blood."

Charles nodded as he continued to observe him carefully. "So, your mother embodies the compassion you long to see in your father, and perhaps in yourself. It is no wonder that your dreams struggle between the two forces. Strength and cruelty on the one hand. Tenderness and mercy on the other. The tension of their union lives within you. Homer, do you think your dreams are urging you to reconcile them."

Homer drew a steady breath, his voice low but resolute. "When I realized I was the lizard in that dream, I felt responsible. It was never just about survival. No, it was more than that. The snake was more than a tricky meal, it was everything I have ever feared would consume me. I could sense the struggle was larger than two creatures locked in combat. It was the same tension that lives everywhere. Between man and woman. In the exchange of power and vulnerability we call love. A father who demands obedience, and a son who longs to breathe on his own terms. The pattern repeats. Master and servant. Employer and worker. Even entire peoples, struggling to remain sovereign while others press to claim them."

He leaned forward, eyes sharp with conviction. "This dream has stirred something within me. Yes, it feels like a warning but also a lesson. It has given me a kind of clarity about life. About risk and reward. Hunger and survival. The way predator and prey live side by side. And the way hero and villain can be the same body."

After taking in a deep breath, he exhaled.

"I've spent so long believing strength meant obedience to appearances. Meanwhile, I was practicing avoidance through sidestepping fear, and enduring quietly. But now I see that turning away only kept me alive in the narrowest sense. If I face what frightens me, truly face it, then perhaps I do not merely persist." Homer offered a faint nod. "Perhaps I can finally claim my life."

Homer fell quiet, the words settling between them like something newly set down.

"A reconciliation," Charles said, gently.

Homer nodded. "Yes, with myself."

Charles did not rush to fill the space. He regarded Homer with a quiet attentiveness, one hand resting loosely around his mug. When he finally spoke, his voice reflected genuine curiosity and a deep respect.

"What you've shared is quite rich, Homer. Symbols like the lizard and the snake, as well as gods and demons, are ancient. In dreams, they are never merely animals," Charles said. "They are expressions, chosen when ordinary language fails."

He leaned back slightly, eyes thoughtful.

"The lizard survives by instincts of alertness when exposed, clinging to warmth and safety where it can find it. The snake, feared and revered in equal measure, carries power: danger, renewal, transformation. The fact you recognized yourself as the lizard tells me something important. You see your own vulnerability. But you also see your endurance. You are not blind to your limits and that awareness itself is a kind of strength."

Homer listened, struck by the ease with which Charles moved through the mindscape of his inner life, as though it were familiar ground. For a brief moment, he wondered if Elsea had spoken to him and possibly shared something personal, some quiet detail from their earlier conversations. The thought passed quickly. He knew she would never betray that trust.

No, he reasoned, this was something else entirely.

Charles seemed to sense what lived beneath words. He read pauses as carefully as speech, noticed the slightest tightening of Homer's jaw, the way his breath changed before certain memories surfaced. It felt less like being analyzed and more like being recognized. As if the man were listening not just with his ears, but with an attunement Homer had never encountered before. At times, it bordered on the uncanny.

And yet, rather than unsettling him, it brought an unexpected calm. For the first time in as long as he could remember, Homer did not feel the need to defend or explain himself. He felt held. Understood. As though some inner door, long closed, had been opened without force.

Chapter Twenty-Eight

"The Shift"

The two scarcely noticed when darkness gave way to twilight. The candle had burned low and been replaced more than once, its small flame bearing quiet witness to the passing hours. Fatigue should have claimed them, yet neither seemed eager to leave the space they had entered together.

This was one of those rare conversations that loosens time's grip in a communion that deepens rather than depletes. Homer spoke with a freedom that surprised even himself, unburdening thoughts he had carried silently for years. Charles, steady and unhurried, listened with a presence that asked nothing and judged nothing, allowing truths to surface in their own time.

What began as the sharing of a dream had become something far more intimate. The good doctor had appeared with a steady hand to perform a careful excavation of meaning, memory, and self. And somewhere in the quiet unfolding of words, Homer sensed a subtle but undeniable shift taking place, not only in understanding, but in the way he inhabited his own life.

For Charles, this moment marked a threshold as well. Until now, his case studies had been assembled at a distance with piecemeal insights gathered through letters, reference books, and lectures offering only fragments of lives observed rather than encountered. Here, however, was a rare gift: to sit across from a young man so raw and unguarded, willing to share not only his mind but the fragile places of his heart, as though each word lifted another stone from the satchel of grief he had carried in silence for far too long.

After describing the events aboard the ship on that fateful morning, how the fog had clung low to the deck and how the sea itself seemed to hold its breath when Robert perished, Homer's composure finally gave way. The telling loosened something long knotted within him, and his tears came suddenly, unrestrained, carrying with them all the grief, guilt, and unspoken terror he had held apart from the world. He made no effort to stop them. For a long while, he could do nothing but breathe and weep, as though his body were carrying grief older than his thoughts, grief that had waited years to be felt.

When at last the storm inside him quieted, Homer reached for the small, weatherworn book he always carried with him. He turned it over in his hands, feeling its familiar weight, his thumb tracing the salt-stained leather as though it might anchor him. The diary was more than paper and ink. It was a refuge, a confessional, a witness. Within its pages lived the parts of himself he had never learned how to speak aloud, his doubts, his fears, the questions that haunted him in the long watches of the night. Everything too fragile or too dangerous for daylight had found its way there, written by lantern glow during countless sleepless hours at sea.

His fingers lingered at the edge of a page marked long ago, trembling despite his effort to still them. He lifted his eyes to Charles. The doctor did not rush him, did not offer counsel or comfort. He simply waited, his presence steady and attentive, the silence between them neither awkward nor empty. In that quiet, Homer realized how rare this moment was and how rarely he had felt so entirely unguarded in another man's company. Trust had taken root between them, slowly and without force, unfolding naturally in the wee small hours of an unforgettable day.

"There's something you should know," Homer said at last, his voice low and rough with emotion. He swallowed, steadying himself. "Something I've never told another soul."

Charles inclined his head, signaling nothing more than that he was listening.

Homer drew a breath and turned the page. He knew the entry by heart, though he had not read it in years. The ink had faded in places, the lines uneven where his hand had shaken as he wrote. Still, the date stood clear at the top of the page, unyielding as a tide mark on stone. There it was, May 21st, 1865:

Last night I was jolted awake by a violent explosion aboard the ship. Just before that horribly tragic moment, I had been deep within a most unusual and troubling dream. In it, I saw toddlers being consumed quite literally by demonic human beings. These children were prepared for the feast beforehand, their small bellies filled with a substance that appeared as liquid gold. I did not intervene. I could only watch as they were guided forward, flowing in silence through a long corridor.

Their final destination, and the manner of their demise, remained unseen. Yet a voice spoke in the background, narrating in a way that left no uncertainty. Whatever presence lingered there was unmistakably evil, consumptive in nature, intent on destruction and taking something that did not belong to it.

The children moved steadily through the corridor. At its entrance stood two adult sentinel beings, one on either side. Their faces were obscured and unrecognizable, as though deliberately withheld from view. The children were naked, save for a simple girdle about their loins, and they passed without resistance, without protest, as though unaware of what awaited them. It seemed as though the children were not seen as children at all, but as vessels, each carrying something to be taken.

The dream filled me with terror and revulsion. I was so disturbed by what I had witnessed that, even within the dream itself, I spoke a humble prayer and begged a higher spirit to remove the vision from my mind. For a moment, I believed it had been granted. Yet soon after, the dream returned to my consciousness, and the voice spoke again. This time instructing me to consider what I had seen from a different perspective. Not literal, it said, but figurative. Not as horror alone, but as symbolic.

I questioned how something so deeply demonic could hold any symbolic meaning at all. In response, the voice spoke plainly, as though explaining something that should have been obvious to me all along:

The corridor is the systems of creation or the ways we come to life.

The children are the innocence that exists in the physical world.

The stomach represents a container that receives the word, the gift, or the light.

The gold is the word, the gifts, and powers of loving light.

The sentinel beings represent the parents of the children and/or those in positions of authority and guidance over the children.

The devouring beings are the demons, those in powerful positions, or even the aspirations and hungers of the world itself.

Charles straightened in his chair, drawing in a slow breath as he absorbed Homer's words. He gave a thoughtful nod before asking, "When you awoke from this dream, what was your first interpretation?"

Homer paused, searching for the words that would not betray the weight of what he felt. "At first," he said, "I believe I was witnessing something deeply menacing. Though I was not physically part of the scene, I could see it unfold and I carried the children's anxiety inside me like it was my own." He hesitated, then continued. "Later, after the boiler explosion, when the door burst open and flames devoured Robert and the others, I began to see the connection. It did not come to me all at once. Only with time and reflection did I understand how closely the dream echoed that horror, how eerily it seemed to anticipate the tragedy that left us adrift at sea for weeks."

Charles lifted his eyes. "In the dream," he asked, "Were the sentient beings nefarious or directly cruel? Did they intend harm toward the children?"

"Not cruel," Homer replied slowly, choosing his words. "They did not act with anger or malice. They treated the children as if they were part of a process, or parts of a product instead of souls, part of humanity." His voice tightened. "They were processed, like ore pulled from the earth, stripping them of their golden pure innocence. I could not see what was beyond the doors where they were led, but the air itself felt poisoned with menace," said Homer.

He considered Homer's words about the sentinels. "You say they were not cruel," he replied. "That is important. Evil in dreams is not always violent. More often it is efficient. Orderly. It wears the face of necessity." He let that thought settle.

"What troubles me," Charles continued softly, "is what was taken from them. Innocence, once given over, cannot be reclaimed in the same form. When such images appear, it is often because something within the dreamer has known this loss already." He paused, then added, almost as an aside, "The psyche does not invent suffering without cause."

Charles studied Homer for a moment before speaking again. "Oftentimes, our dreams are a result from experiences in our own lives, which might be a derivative of the interplay between our conscious and subconscious mind," continued Charles. "Deeply rooted feelings and viewpoints can be manifested into visual symbols of thoughts and emotions playing out during our dream state. It is truly fascinating how our minds process information. We've barely begun understanding the scope of the human brain and its different parts that are interconnected with our consciousness."

Homer leaned forward slightly and asked, "Do you mean somewhere in my life I felt these feelings from an experience and they were shown within my dream?" Charles adjusted slightly, his voice measured. "Oftentimes our dreams arise from experiences buried deep within us, the fragments of life woven together with our body's carbon chemistry and manifesting between the conscious and the subconscious. What you describe as the stripping away of innocence, the processing of life as though it were a mere product may echo not only the boiler tragedy but other wounds you carry."

He studied Homer for a moment before asking quietly, "Tell me, Homer… have you ever felt treated in such a way yourself? Processed rather than seen?"

Charles let a moment pass, knowing the next question would cut a little deeper. He did not rush it. Then, carefully he asked, "By the Navy, perhaps? By your own family?" Then, gently but unavoidably:

"By your father?"

Homer's face tightened, his eyes clouding as memories surfaced. "Captain Marcus... yes. He demanded I take to whaling life, pressed me into a trade I despised. He treated me less like a son, more like an heir to his bloody legacy. I can still hear his voice, hard as iron, telling me I had no choice but to follow his path." Charles nodded slowly, as if fitting puzzle pieces together. "And your first hunt? What do you recall of that moment?"

Homer swallowed hard, his voice rough. "The whale's death. The spray of blood against the sea. The great body thrashing, the cries echoing across the waves as the harpoons struck. That sight was seared into me. I remember wanting to turn away, but my father's hand gripped my shoulder, forcing me to watch. That was the day innocence left me."

Charles regarded him with profound sadness. "Then perhaps the dream is not only about the children or the explosion so much as it may be about you, Homer. The child pressed into a corridor not of his choosing, guided by the sentinels of authority, and made to witness death until his innocence was consumed. These are archetypal images drawn from the deepest layers of your psyche." Homer exhaled slowly, his voice tinged with wonder. "I just have to find out what thoughts or experiences are causing me to dream such dreams?"

Charles leaned back, his tone warm and steady. "That search is important, Homer. But remember, dreams are not meant to trouble us. They can serve as teachers, carrying fragments of memory, pain, even hope, into forms we can begin to understand. You are already showing the courage to face them, which is more than most men ever attempt. My counsel is this: do not burden yourself with the need to solve them all at once. Instead, let them guide you as you continue living with openness and reflection. What matters most is that you honor both the questions and the experiences shaping you."

He studied Homer for a moment, his eyes kind but searching. "If you are willing," he said, "we can begin where the sea did not reach. There are stories the body remembers long before the mind allows them room. If you ever choose to speak them, you need not do so alone."

Homer nodded and leafed through the pages of his diary until he found the date, July 10th, 1865. He lingered there, breathing in slowly, as though steadying himself.

"Are you all right, Homer?" Charles asked gently.

"Yes," Homer replied. "I began writing this entry a few days ago, but I couldn't continue. What happened an hour before... I couldn't bring myself to put it on paper. It felt unbelievable, even as it was happening." He hesitated. "I've never told anyone what occurred that morning. It was too personal, too shameful and miraculous all at once."

"Doctor Young," he began.

"Please," Charles said calmly, interrupting with a small smile. "My friends call me Charles."

Homer returned the smile and continued.

"In the darkest hours before sunrise," he said, "after we paid tribute to Robert and the two others lost in the fire, we shared the last of our rum. We knew then we might not survive the open sea." His voice faltered. "I was overwhelmed with feeling physically broken, mentally exhausted. For the first time in my life, I felt utterly hopeless. I wanted only for the pain to end. I reached a tipping point I'm not proud of, and one I've never spoken aloud." His eyes filled. "I meant to surrender myself to the sea. I meant to drown."

"There is no shame in speaking this truth," Charles said quietly. "To endure despair and still live to tell of it is the mark of one who has already faced death and returned. You are here now. Alive. Present. Courageous for naming what you once carried alone."

"That's just it," Homer said. "I did throw myself into the ocean. I tried to end it." He swallowed hard. "As I floated in the restless water and watched the ship drift farther away, I knew there was no turning back. Even if I wanted to save myself, I no longer could. Instinct took over. I fought the currents, struggled to stay afloat but exhaustion claimed me. I began to take in water. I remember crying out from somewhere deep within, help me… please help me, knowing all the while there was no one there to hear."

His hands trembled. Charles reached across the table and clasped them gently. "Take your time," he said. "Tell me what came next, only if you are ready."

"I'm all right," Homer replied softly. "I believed I was completely alone. I thought of my mother and how much sorrow my death would bring her. My siblings. Most importantly my thoughts turned to Noko." His voice tightened. "Then I thought of my father, how disappointed he would be, how he would see my act as cowardice." He paused. "I thought I was alone. But I wasn't."

He drew a breath and released slowly as if passing his breath with his thoughts.

"Just as I began to sink beneath the surface, something nudged me upward. At first, I thought I was being attacked. Then I realized exactly who it was. The pod of whales we had seen earlier that day. We had watched them play alongside the ship, breaching and splashing us in the light. I recognized the elder female. I'd seen her before while standing watch. It sounds strange, but it felt like I knew her."

Charles remained silent, offering only his attention.

"Before I could understand what was happening," Homer continued, "the pod formed a circle around me. I felt myself lifted from the water, resting upon the broad head of the largest whale. They carried me toward the ship, which was nearly lost to the horizon by then. We moved so swiftly I could hardly comprehend it. For a moment, I believed I had already died and that this was some final mercy of the mind."

He swallowed, his throat feeling dry.

"But as we drew near, the great whale thrust me upward with a force I cannot describe. I summoned the last of my strength, hauled myself over the rail, and collapsed onto the deck. The pain I felt upon impact told me this was no dream. It was real. "His voice softened. "When I looked back, the pod lingered. And when my eyes met those of the mother whale, I felt something I had never known before. A love so vast and fierce it pierced my very soul."

For a long moment, Charles said nothing. At last, he drew a slow, deliberate breath.

"Homer," he said, "what you experienced was more than chance. Few men are carried back from the abyss. Those whales did not merely lift your body from the sea, they carried your spirit back from despair, entrusted with meaning. You must consider that rescue as more than survival, it could very well be a sign."

"A sign of what?" Homer asked with curiosity.

"That life has claimed you still," Charles replied. "That love, whether it be divine, natural, or born from the mysteries of the deep, has chosen not to abandon you. You felt it in the eye of the mother whale, did you not?"

"Yes," Homer said. "As if she knew me. As if she forgave me."

"Do not dismiss that love as chance," Charles said. "It was a gift, perhaps from creation itself, meant to remind you that your life is bound to something greater than mere survival. When a man's own heart turns against him, when despair convinces him he is alone, creation itself sometimes rises to say otherwise."

He leaned closer, his voice steady and sure. "Those whales stand for strength, endurance, and belonging, for all who could not reach you: your mother, your siblings, even the father whose shadow you still wrestle with. Where human hands failed, nature's hand prevailed. You were meant to live, Homer. And you were meant to be changed by that love."

His voice lowered. "Your life is no longer yours to cast away. It has been returned to you, shaped by trial, and preserved with purpose. That is the burden, and the gift, of a hero."

Homer hesitated. "And what of the world's hunger and the demons that seek to consume what is good? How does the hero protect the golden gift from being devoured?"

Charles considered this, then spoke softly. "That is the trial of every true hero. The world will always contain demons, some wearing crowns, others hiding within the heart. Their hunger is to strip the soul of its light, to turn the golden gift into fuel for their own appetite. But the hero's task is not to flee them. It is to guard the gift, to tend it, and to wield it for good."

After a brief pause Charles continued, “You protect it by knowing its worth. By refusing to let the world reduce you to material or machinery. The light grows stronger when it is shared, when it becomes a lamp for others. A hero resists not only for himself, but so that others might remember their own light. That is how the gift endures, even in the shadow of demons.”

Just then, Elsea moved quietly through the room, blew out the candle, and opened the tavern window shade. Morning light spilled in. “Well then,” she said warmly, “what are we having for breakfast on this fine morning, my loves?”

Chapter Twenty-Nine

"A New Day"

Both Charles and Homer shared an early breakfast with light, friendly conversation. It was not about dreams, the subconscious, or any of the tender places they had entered together during the night. Charles could see in Homer's face and posture how fatigue sat behind his eyes and in his body. He sensed the young man needed sleep more than further unraveling, and he knew the moment would sour if forced. For now, it was simply two men at a tavern table who had, in the quiet hours, become something like friends.

From the kitchen came the steady sounds of Elsea beginning her morning preparation routine, the clink of utensils, the soft scrape of a chair, the faint hum of movement. It was a welcome sign of a new day. The sun had only just crested the horizon, and to Homer it felt like a reminder that the world kept turning even after fire, grief, and confession. He felt blessed to be alive, and grateful for Charles, for the calm presence he offered, and for insight into questions Homer had carried so long he had forgotten what it felt like to set them down. He realized it had begun months earlier with a chance meeting, when he discovered Elsea's kindness, her steady regard, her unspoken invitation to return to himself.

Elsea approached their table and looked at them both with the same practical affection she had offered since the beginning.

"Gentlemen," she said, sincere but stern, "it's time you head to your respective quarters and get some well-earned rest."

Both men knew any counter would be futile. They nodded in agreement, almost in unison.

"She's right," Charles admitted with a tired smile. "I'm worn out myself."

They pushed their chairs back and stood. Homer extended his hand, and Charles met it with a firm shake. Homer's voice caught, the feeling in his throat arriving before language.

"Charles… I don't have the words right now," he said. "So I'll just say thank you. From the bottom of my heart, thank you."

Charles grinned, as if to keep the moment from becoming too heavy. "And I thank you as well," he replied. "It's been a pleasure."

Within minutes Homer was in the very room Elsea had set him up with many months ago when he first visited the Tavern Inn. He stumbled to the water closet and washed up before heading to bed and fell into a deep sleep. He slept through the morning and into early afternoon. When he woke, it took him a moment to remember where he was. There were no dreams that clung to him, nor any perilous thoughts racing through his head.

He exhaled, then inhaled again, repeating the slow rhythm until his bearings returned. It was as if he was soaking in all that had materialized over the past day while reflecting on the confession, the listening, the release. A smile came over him as the sunlight peaked through the shear curtains. It was a smile that represented relief and fresh starts. Homer had not understood the depth of the burden his thoughts and dreams had placed upon him over the years. It had taken a stranger who became a friend in the wee small hours of the night, and a conversation that eased a weight he had been carrying for years, to show him how heavy he had been living.

Mostly, he felt grateful for his friendships with Charles and Elsea, and for understanding of his thoughts, dreams, and feelings he never imagined sharing with anyone beyond Noko. He walked to the window and welcomed the sight of the ocean and the growing bustle of the port below. Standing there, he lingered on the water's vastness, its steady motion and shifting light, knowing he would never look upon it in quite the same way again.

As a young boy, the ocean had been a place of joy and motion, where he and his childhood friends splashed in the shallows, cast their lines, and disappeared into long summer afternoons. During adolescence, it took on a heavier presence, becoming a place of beauty layered with unease, where mystery and sorrow lived close together and he first understood how easily wonder can give way to harm. His years in the Navy deepened that understanding further, revealing the vastness of the world and the many forces, human, natural, and unseen, that quietly shape a life. What once felt contained now felt expansive, and within that widening view, he sensed that new beginnings were still possible.

After spending time simply taking it all in, Homer washed, dressed, and headed out to see what the day would hold. He felt invigorated and strangely light, as if he had stepped out of an old coat he did not realize he'd been wearing. He reminded himself to let the day unfold instead of worrying over what must be done. The smell of sea air energized his senses. As he strolled along the wharf, he noticed with surprise that the pain in his back and hip had subsided, as though some inner knot had loosened and the body had followed.

He remembered where the wounded ship had docked and walked toward it. The very vessel that limped back to port after battling dire moments with the crew sat solemnly now and was being used for sleeping quarters and mostly storage until repairs were attempted, or it would be broken down and sold for scrap. Homer was optimistic about the former. He wanted to see it made whole, not reduced to pieces and profit.

As he approached the ship, there were a few men surveying the damage and talking with Captain Adams. Homer saluted him as he walked by, not wanting to interrupt their conversation. He headed down the hall toward his quarters with a different mindset than previously; the echoes of loss from Robert hit him differently now as he was at peace with all that had taken place on the ship throughout his fateful journey.

He thought of Robert as a hero. A man who never backed away from a challenge. A man who would not want pity. Homer knew, with sudden certainty, that Robert would not want his bunkmate to carry sorrow like chains.

The smell of his dorm was dank and familiar, and it brought with it a rush of memories of all that had taken place within the confines of both the ship and this birthing space. Homer realized how much he missed being out at sea and the early morning chats with Robert. He reached for his journal and began writing:

Last night I received what felt like answers to some questions I yearned to understand, and some I did not realize needed answering. I always knew I held so many things inside me that were perplexing but was fearful to delve deeper into why I felt the way I did, why I dreamt of the things I dreamt, and what this all meant. Now I realize that there lies a certain mystery in some occurrences in this life, and we may not ever know, but I do know I am meant to follow my heart and keep an open mind while on this journey. I feel a sense of weightlessness I have not felt since I was a young boy. I no longer feel the need to control those things that I truly have no control over in the first place. I am awake, alive, and in tune with this beautiful place in which we live. I look forward to my return home and cannot wait to see my family again, my friends, and Noko.

Homer closed his journal and placed it beside his copy of Moby-Dick within his satchel and made a mental note to continue reading the novel he had put down weeks ago when he and the crew were in survival mode. He reminisced about the town bookstore, the afternoon with Elsea, and how the book had found its way into his hands at exactly the right time.

Then he decided he ought to speak with Captain Adams. The meeting with the other men had ended, and Homer spotted the captain on deck. He approached with a steadier heart than he would have had yesterday.

"Captain, Sir, may I have a quick word with you?" he asked politely.

"Of course, Deep, I've been looking forward to catching up with you as well. What's on your mind sailor?" as he shook Homer's hand firmly.

"Sir, I realize how much I miss my home and family, and considering all that has taken place…"

Captain Adams met eyes with Homer and grinned with warmth. "Deep, say no more. I respectfully believe your time with the Navy has been served well, and you have my blessing for an honorable discharge."

There was an audible exhale of relief from Homer, "Thank you, sir. I was having trouble getting the words out and you already knew what I was thinking, I'm sure."

Captain Adams replied, "Son, it's been well-deserved, and I will see to it that the proper papers are in order for you."

Relief washed over Homer, quiet and complete.

Chapter Thirty

"Northbound"

The word son lingered longer than anything else Captain Adams had said.

It settled in Homer's chest with an unfamiliar weight, not heavy exactly, but present, like something placed carefully where it had always been missing. Captain Adams had become more than a commanding officer over the years. He had been a steady hand, a voice of order in chaos, a man who understood when to speak and when to let silence do the work. In this quiet moment of departure, he felt closer to a father than Homer had known in a very long while.

Homer realized how long it had been since anyone had called him son. Not since the day he boarded the ship, and even then the word had come from his mother, spoken softly and with worry as she stood at the edge of the dock. His father had not said it and at the time Homer really did not expect him to. The absence of that single word had shaped more of Homer's life than he ever understood. He felt it now and how much he had missed it, how deeply he had carried that absence without naming it.

It brought an unexpected smile to his face.

Standing there, with the dock beneath his boots and the ship quiet behind him, Homer found himself thinking of how certain people enter a life briefly yet alter its course forever. Dr. Young, whom he had met by chance in the late hours of a sleepless night, had shifted something fundamental within him. Through Dr. Young's careful listening and unhurried questions, Homer had been offered a new way of seeing not only himself, but his father as well.

Captain Marcus no longer stood in his memory as a singular antagonist. He was still stern, still unyielding, but now Homer could see the shape of the man beneath the command, a life forged by expectation, by survival, by a world that did not reward lackluster ambition. In this new light, Homer could hold both Captain Marcus and Captain Adams in the same frame: men of strength and stoicism, alike in discipline, yet vastly different in how they offered guidance. One ruled through force of will, the other through steadiness and regard.

It had taken a stranger's voice to open that understanding. Homer felt no bitterness in the realization, only clarity. He knew, standing there, that when he returned home he would seek a different kind of conversation with his father. Not one rooted in resistance or old wounds, but in honesty. He felt ready for it. More than that, he wanted it.

Captain Adams stepped closer and pressed a small, weathered silver coin into Homer's palm. The metal was cool, an image of the Pawnee etched on the surface, its edges worn smooth by years of handling.

"This is to remember your service," Adams said. "*To The Pawnee* and to the Navy."

Homer closed his fingers around the token with a recognition of pride and the honor it held.

"Thank you, sir," he replied. "I'll carry her memory with me." Homer slipped the coin into his pocket, feeling its weight settle there as though it had always belonged.

As he turned away from the ship, the salt air filled his lungs. It felt as familiar as breath itself, like a language his body spoke fluently, even if he would not be speaking it every day anymore. The ship remained behind him now, quiet and wounded, but no longer holding him in place. They let each other go.

He sensed it before he saw her.

Elsea stood above the dock, her presence unmistakable. It was the same sensation he had felt the day the crew first staggered back into port. Her gaze always seemed to find him without effort, as though the world naturally arranged itself that way. No words were needed. He knew where to look. He knew she would be there and he took comfort in that reassurance.

Moments later, Charles joined them, his coat drawn close against the breeze, the collar turned up as though he were only just becoming aware of the cold. The night had left its mark on him; there was a faint heaviness in his posture, a measured deliberateness to his steps that spoke of hours spent listening rather than sleeping. Yet when he looked up, his eyes were clear and steady, carrying none of the blur that comes from exhaustion alone.

He offered them a small, knowing smile, the kind that acknowledged both the lateness of the hour and the conversation that had preceded it. Charles then settled beside them without hurry. There was something unspoken in the way he arrived, as though he had stepped into the moment itself and into its aftermath, content to see whatever remained rather than reopen what had already passed.

They began the walk toward the train station together.

The streets were already alive with horses snorting softly as carriages passed, the clatter of hooves on stone, the low hum of voices beginning their day. Their conversation stayed light, almost deliberately so. Small observations. Brief laughter. The kind of talk that acknowledges what has already been shared and does not need to revisit it.

Perhaps none of them wished to weigh the moment down with ceremony. Homer understood now that some connections are diminished when explained too thoroughly. What had passed between them would endure without being spoken again.

The station platform smelled of coal and leather, somehow reminding him of Robert. When the black locomotive came into view, steam hissing into the cool morning air, Homer felt a quiet shift within himself. He would be trading the rhythm of tides for the rhythm of iron and rail. It felt strange but easily acceptable.

Beyond the tracks, trees stood heavy with autumn color, leaves glowing in shades of amber and rust. A memory stirred, and there arose scenes of jumping into piles of fallen leaves back home, laughter echoing through crisp air. He had not thought of that in years.

Captain Adams appeared once more, greeting Elsea and Charles before turning to Homer. He handed him a weathered satchel.

"These belonged to Robert," he said. "Arrangements have been made for you to stop in Boston and deliver them to his family."

Homer felt the weight of the satchel immediately. It was not heavy in mass, but in meaning. He nodded.

"It would be my honor, sir."

"I don't care for goodbyes," Elsea said, her voice warm but firm. "So I'll say until we meet again."

"I'll write, I promise," Homer said.

Elsea paused for a moment, being sure to look into Homer's eyes, "I will do the same. I have always wanted a penpal."

Charles clasped his hand. "Keep reading," he said quietly. "Keep writing. And keep noticing what you once overlooked."

The train's horn sounded signaling ten minutes before departure.

They parted without spectacle, each stepping back into their own current.

Homer paused at the threshold of the carriage, one hand resting briefly on the iron rail, as if acknowledging the moment before it passed him by. He boarded the train with wide eyes. He had never ridden one before, and the interior struck him with its careful craftsmanship. Homer appreciated the polished wood, brass fittings, a quiet dignity that felt almost ceremonial. As he found his seat, he was greeted by William Bowditch, a senior officer from the ship. Bowditch was known by sailors as "a lifer," married to the sea. Soon he would receive command of his own vessel.

"I'll accompany you as far as Boston," Bowditch said.

Homer thanked him, and when the train lurched forward, he felt the difference immediately. The sea yielded. The rail did not. The motion ran straight through his spine. The force was unyielding, directional, decisive. His body instinctively searched for the familiar roll of water beneath him, but there was none. Only forward movement. The sound of the wheels steadied him in a way he did not expect.

As the harbor fell away, Homer reached into his satchel and drew out the obsidian stone Noko had given him the night before he left for the Navy. It rested cool and smooth in his palm, catching faint glints of light as the landscape slipped past the window. He turned it slowly, noticing hues of black, gold, and silver he had never truly seen before.

He thought of Noko and wondered if she would recognize him. Their love, born from friendship and adventure, was a presence that had traveled with him even across distance and silence. The stone she had given him felt alive in his grasp, as though it carried its own memory.

He opened his journal and wrote:

The smaller the stone, the more distant the memory. Yet even the smallest detail can call back an entire world.

The steady rhythm of the train carried him into a light, untroubled sleep.

Chapter Thirty-One

"Fair Winds and Farewells"

Boston arrived beneath a sky washed clean by rain, the clouds thinning into pale streaks as if the city itself were exhaling. The slowing of the train stirred Homer from a light, untroubled sleep. For a moment, he did not know where he was, only that he felt rested in a way that surprised him. The rhythm beneath his body had changed again, no longer the roll of waves nor the steady hum of the open rail, but something gentler, final.

Officer Bowditch stood in the aisle, adjusting his coat with the practiced precision of a man shaped by command and habit.

"Looks like we have arrived," he said.

Homer blinked, sitting upright. "I'm afraid I slept through half the view."

Bowditch smiled faintly. "Boston's a fine city. You'll see it just fine."

They gathered their belongings and disembarked together. The platform glistened with rain, and the air smelled of iron, wet stone, and fallen leaves crushed underfoot. Autumn had taken hold here with intention, maples flaring red and gold, their leaves skittering across cobblestone like sparks stirred by wind. Homer paused at the edge of the platform, letting the city announce itself before stepping fully into it.

At the station's edge, the two men shook hands. The gesture was firm, unceremonious, complete.

"Fair winds," Bowditch said.

"And following seas, sir." Homer replied.

As Bowditch turned back toward the train, Homer unfolded the note bearing Robert's address. The paper was creased and softened by handling, as though it had already traveled far before reaching his hands. A few locals helped him along the way, some offering hurried directions, others lingering long enough to be sure he understood, until he found his way through the city streets. The walk steadied him. Each step brought a quiet resolve, the satchel at his side heavy with both duty and remembrance.

The house stood at last before him: modest, Tudor in style, with a brick walkway bordered by meticulously tended roses. The garden struck him immediately. Someone had cared for this place attentively, season after season, regardless of weather or fortune.

He rapped his knuckles against the door with firm, deliberate force, the kind of knock learned at sea, unapologetic and unmistakable, meant to be heard above wind and surf. The sound echoed briefly through the house, solid and final, and Homer stepped back a half pace to wait. He squared his shoulders, resting his weight evenly on his boots, eyes fixed on the worn wood as the seconds stretched, listening for movement beyond the threshold.

Robert's father, Carl Brown, opened the door. He stood upright, shoulders squared, his eyes steady but worn by something deeper than fatigue. After brief introductions, Homer was welcomed inside.

Warmth met him at once. Homer could hear the crackle of a fire, the soft ticking of a clock, the low hum of a house that still carried life within it. Carl moved with measured restraint, his gestures economical, his words chosen with care. Homer sensed a lifetime of work behind him, a man who had learned to let actions speak louder than explanations. He saw Robert in him immediately.

Mrs. Brown joined them shortly after, her presence calm, her voice gentle but composed. Tea was poured. A simple meal was prepared. The ordinariness of the moment, the placement of cups, the careful passing of plates, felt unexpectedly reverent. Grief lived here, but it did not dominate. It had been made room for, and nothing more.

When the moment felt right, Homer opened the satchel. He placed the locket, the folded letter, and the small journal on the table between them. His hands did not shake.

"I'm so sorry for your loss," he said quietly. "Robert was the spirit of our ship. My best friend."

Mrs. Brown nodded slowly, her eyes glistening. "We're grateful he had you."

Carl cleared his throat and spoke of duty and sacrifice, of the sea's toll and the pride that often accompanies it. When he finished, he reached into a drawer and placed a small wooden carving into Homer's hand. It was a whale, smoothed by years of touch.

"He always said you could hear what others couldn't," Carl said. "The quiet between storms."

The words settled with a quiet gravity. Homer closed his fingers around the carving, feeling its weight and the smooth patience worn into it by time and touch. In that small object, he sensed not only Robert's presence, but the steadiness of a family who understood loss and carried it with dignity.

When he rose to leave, he reached out instinctively to offer his hand, the familiar courtesy of a guest preparing to depart. Instead, the Browns stepped forward and drew him into their arms. The embrace came without hesitation or formality, firm and sure, as though it required no explanation. In their closeness, Homer felt something shift within him, a brief but undeniable sense of belonging. For a moment, he was not a visitor delivering memories, but someone received and held as one of their own. The warmth of it lingered even after they released him, settling deep enough to carry with him when he stepped back out into the day.

Outside, the afternoon light had softened, the sharpness of the day giving way to a gentler hue that settled over the street and the garden alike. The roses along the brick path stirred in a passing breeze, their petals trembling as though aware of the parting taking place. Homer lingered at the threshold, reluctant to step fully away, carrying with him the warmth of the house and the quiet dignity that lived within its walls.

Carl walked with him to the door and rested a hand briefly on the frame, his gaze drifting toward the distant line of the harbor. "There's a place," he said at last, his voice low and measured, "where Robert used to go when the sea grew heavy on him. Not often. Only when he needed stillness." He paused, choosing his words with care. "A small chapel near Salem. Overlooks the water. It helped him listen to the voice within when the world grew loud."

Homer nodded, understanding without needing further

explanation. The address was not written down and no directions were given. Carl simply gestured toward the coast, trusting that Homer would find it. With a final handshake that was firm and deliberate, its meaning left unspoken, Homer stepped away. The weight of the day settled differently now, guided by the quiet knowledge that some places are not meant to be sought, but answered.

Homer walked there alone, his steps steady and unhurried, the sound of them softened by the narrow road and the wind off the water. Yet with each turn and each familiar scent of salt and damp earth, he felt Robert beside him in a way that required no effort of imagination. It was not a figure he saw or a voice he heard, but a presence carried in memory and muscle, in the shared habits formed over long days at sea.

He noticed small details as though through Robert's awareness, the angle of the light along the shoreline, the rise of gulls against the sky, the widening of the horizon where the land fell away. At moments, he found himself waiting for a quiet remark, the kind that would have come naturally between them. The silence that followed did not feel empty. It felt familiar, companionable, able to keep pace without asking anything in return.

Though he walked by himself, he did not feel alone. Robert's presence moved with him, not as something held tightly, but as something carried forward, folded gently into the rhythm of his steps as he continued on.

The chapel stood overlooking the harbor, its modest wooden frame set against the wide expanse of water beyond. Years of weather had softened its lines, the boards worn to a pale gray, yet every joint and beam bore the mark of steady care. Nothing about the place sought attention. It endured through quiet maintenance, repaired when necessary, left undisturbed when not.

A steady wind moved through the grass surrounding it, bending the blades in slow, deliberate waves. The air carried the unmistakable scent of salt and kelp, the Atlantic's breath drifting inland as if the sea itself lingered nearby, attentive but unannounced. From where he stood, Homer heard the distant cry of gulls and the muted percussion of water striking pilings below, a low, constant rhythm that echoed the shoreline.

He paused at the threshold, resting one hand lightly against the door. The wood felt cool beneath his palm, smooth from years of touch. When he stepped inside, he did so with care, his boots sounding softly against the age-smoothed boards. Each footfall seemed absorbed by the floor, as though the space were listening rather than responding.

Light filtered through the stained glass, settling across the pews in quiet bands of color with dusty blues, softened golds, a faint wash of red. The light arrived without announcement, falling exactly where it belonged. Homer stood still, allowing his eyes to adjust, his breathing to slow, the hush of the chapel to gather around him.

Then he lifted his gaze.

His breath caught.

The beams overhead curved inward with a deliberate grace, rising and meeting one another in a form that felt less constructed than grown. They were neither ornamental nor imposing, but purposeful, holding the ceiling the way a body holds breath almost instinctively, without strain. Their rib-like arc enclosed the space with a quiet geometry, creating the unmistakable sensation of being inside something rather than merely beneath it.

Homer felt it before he gave it language. The space carried a sense of containment that asked nothing of him, a holding that required no effort or resistance. The ceiling no longer read as timber and joinery alone. It became a vast interior, familiar in a way he could not immediately place.

As the recognition settled, his body responded as he noticed his shoulders eased, his chest loosened, his breath deepened, as though he had entered a place where breathing itself was remembered. The chapel curved around him like the interior of a great living form, shaped for endurance and stillness alike. In that moment, understanding arrived without force.

The structure carried the quiet logic of a vessel shaped by long acquaintance with the sea. It seemed accustomed to depth, motion, and pressure without yielding to them. Standing there, Homer sensed the world settle rather than press upon him. The sound softened. Time had widened. The urgency of the surface receded until it no longer demanded his attention.

For a long moment, he remained beneath those ribs, suspended between land and ocean, past and present, as something ancient stirred within him, arriving as recognition.

Memory followed as images more than sensation. He imagined the vast interior of a whale: the slow, steady rhythm of life beneath the waves, the way sound travels differently there, the way time stretches and folds inward. The beams above him became the frame of a living sanctuary, and the air itself felt borrowed from the sea.

Only then did he understand why this place had mattered to Robert.

Homer knelt and placed Robert's name into the parish book. The stillness pressed close without being heavy, nor demanding, but complete. Somewhere, an organ chimed softly, its low hum resonating through the wood. It reminded him of whale song, the sounds vibrating deep within his chest. It felt like something ancient. Something calling without urgency.

Warmth spread through him. Peace followed. Homer's countenance was all aglow.

Before leaving, he stepped toward the altar. His fingers brushed the polished wood.

"May the tide carry your soul gently," he whispered.

Twilight had begun its slow descent when Homer returned to the street. He walked back toward the station unhurried, allowing the world to move around him. Autumn deepened with each step, the colors rich and deliberate, as though the land itself were preparing for rest.

The train carried him north once more, its iron wheels striking the rails with a steady cadence that traveled up through the floor and into his bones. The compartment rocked gently beneath him, a familiar motion now, neither jarring nor lulling, just enough to remind him that he was in motion. Outside the window, the land slipped past in long, unbroken stretches, fields giving way to trees, trees opening briefly onto water before closing again.

Coal smoke drifted back along the cars, sharp and metallic in the air, mingling with the scent of polished wood and worn leather inside the carriage. Sunlight flashed and faded as the train passed through pockets of shade, illuminating dust motes that hovered briefly before settling again. Voices murmured somewhere down the aisle, boots shifted, a latch rattled and stilled.

Homer let the rhythm take him. He rested his head back against the seat, feeling the vibration of the engine and the pull of distance closing behind him. With each mile, the north drew nearer, not as a destination alone, but as a continuation of the path already set in motion.

America unfolded beyond the glass with endless fields and rivers, towns stitched together by track and smoke. Homer felt an unexpected affection for the land, not born of command or declaration, but of continuity. Sea and soil, movement and stillness, each shaping the other. Passengers came and went: mothers, laborers, children, dreamers. He sensed a shared rhythm among them, a nation breathing through countless lives moving forward.

He opened his journal and wrote:

The land breathes as the sea does, with rhythm, patience, and purpose. To care for one is to honor the other.

Twilight thickened. Marine mist gathered along the tracks. Forests marbled orange and shadow. Homer added one final line before closing his journal:

Whether beneath waves or over rails, the current carries us all home.

He rested the obsidian stone in his palm, its surface cool and smooth against his skin. The dark sheen caught what little light remained, blurring his reflection until it became indistinct, with sky dissolving into sea, memory drifting into the present, and love settling gently into longing. The stone felt steady and unchanging, as though it had been waiting for his hand to still long enough to notice it.

He turned it slowly, watching the world shift across its surface. Faces appeared and vanished. Places passed through it without settling. In its depth, he sensed strength in continuity, a reminder that what is carried does not always announce itself, and what endures often does so quietly.

Beyond the window, the landscape moved in long, unbroken lines. The train pressed forward with patient resolve, its rhythm neither hurried nor hesitant. Homer allowed himself to follow it, feeling the motion ease something tight within him. For the first time in longer than he could remember, the forward pull did not feel like escape.

As the train carried him onward, a feeling rose that surprised him in its simplicity. It was not urgency, nor anticipation sharpened by fear. It was a clean, steady excitement, the kind that comes not from leaving something behind, but from moving toward what has always been waiting.

It was not the sharp surge that comes from fleeing what has grown unbearable. It was a pull that did not rush him forward but drew him steadily on. Homer felt it in the even rhythm of the train, in the way his breath matched its pace, in the calm certainty that he was moving toward something familiar rather than away from something unresolved.

This motion carried no urgency, no need to outrun the past. Instead, it gathered the pieces of his journey and held them together as he traveled on. What awaited him was not untouched or idealized, but real, shaped by memory and time, ready to be met again. And in that steady movement, unhurried and assured, Homer recognized the simple truth he had been circling all along.

He was not running.

He was returning.

Chapter Thirty-Two

"Currents leading Home"

"Ready the starboard lines for our port approach!" the skipper of the jolly boat barked.

The command snapped through the salt air, and for an instant Homer was back aboard the Pawnee, standing at his station and braced for whatever the sea demanded of him next. As the jolly boat eased toward Newport harbor, Homer felt the weight of everything he had carried rising inside him, everything layered and pressing against his ribs: the deaths he had witnessed, the darkness he had wandered through, the moments that nearly claimed his life, and the rare, fragile moments that pulled him back toward living. Nearly two years at sea had reshaped him in ways the boy who first left home could have never imagined.

The boat glided through the morning harbor, its tired sails fluttering with a kind of final breath. Shoreline chimneys released thin ribbons of smoke that drifted lazily across the rooftops, and the scent of burning wood mingled with the familiar tang of salt. Homer watched the coastline draw nearer, every foot of distance closing the space between who he had become and who he expected his family believed him to be.

He felt the subtle shift beneath his feet as the deckhands called to one another and the crew prepared to dock. The sea had carried him for so long that the idea of standing on unmoving ground he called home felt almost foreign. He braced himself not just for the earth's firmness, but for the return to a world that had continued without him.

When the gangway was finally set into place and Homer stepped onto the dock, the boards creaked beneath his boots with a sound that felt almost like greeting. He paused for a moment, allowing the air to fill his lungs. It carried the cool sharpness of early autumn and the faint sweetness of distant hearth fires so familiar, grounding, and disquieting all at once.

Newport's shoreline bustled with fishermen unloading their morning catch, merchants sweeping the fronts of their shops, and gulls circling overhead in their repetitive, hungry arcs. Life here had kept its rhythm, steady and uninterested in the storms he had survived. And yet, stepping into that rhythm felt like stepping into a memory he had outgrown.

Homer adjusted the strap of his weathered seabag over his shoulder and began walking toward town. Each footstep felt like a test: of who he had been, who he had become, and who he still feared he might be. Behind him, the memory of the Pawnee settled heavily against the dock of his heart, and for the first time he felt the ship no longer needed him. He knew she was in good hands with her captain and crew.

Ahead, Newport waited in its quiet coastal way, unaware of the man returning to its streets, unaware of the whale who had once died and been reborn inside him, unaware of the storms he had carried back to shore. And Homer, with his heart full of the truths he had gathered at sea, stepped forward. As his feet met solid ground, for a fleeting moment the earth seemed to tilt beneath him feeling the sway of the sea still alive in his bones.

He filled his lungs deeply, feeling the cold carve through him. The breath shuddered on the way out, carrying the residue of shipboard air and salt-slick memory. His fingers flexed at his sides in a sort of sailor's ritual, grounding himself in the solidity of land. The sea, once an adversary, now seemed to hum beneath it all like a pulse he carried within his ribs. He looked down at the sand, the same grains he'd walked as a boy, and something swelled within his chest. It was neither grief nor joy but something older than both: the ache of remembering a love long recognized.

Arriving at the beach where he and Noko played, he walked toward the water's edge and crouched, letting the surf rush over his boots. The cold bit through the leather, creeping up his ankles, with a tingling that felt like little ants climbing along his leg. He smiled faintly.

"You haven't changed," he murmured to the sea. "But I have."

The obsidian stone lay warm in his pocket. He placed it atop the small rock cairn he and Noko had built long ago, marking a promise kept. The stone glimmering darkly in the low sun, swallowing light and returning it as a single glint of fire.

As he stood, the smell of home carried up the dunes with smoke, damp cedar, and the faint sweetness of baking bread. Each inhalation stirred memories like embers rekindling: his mother's humming, the low rumble of his father's voice, the soft laughter of siblings echoing through cottage walls. His stomach clenched with anticipation and maybe a little fear.

He walked the familiar road, sand turning to packed dirt beneath his feet. With every step, his heart beat harder. He rolled his shoulders in an attempt to ease the tension, but it clung stubbornly. His mind rehearsed the moment he'd see his father and whether it would be a nod, a word, or silence. Captain Marcus's voice, stern and measured, lived in his head like an old captain barking orders. Homer's body remembered too sensing the stiff spine, the held breath, the way love had once hidden behind obedience.

By the time he reached the door, his palms were slick.

Then his mother's laughter rang from within the cottage walls, a melody so warm and familiar it seemed to reach straight into his chest, softening the tempests that churned within him. When she opened the door and saw him, her cry cut through the stillness like the foghorn of the Pawnee. Her arms wrapped around him before he could speak, and he let the sound of her heartbeat fill his ears. His shoulders dropped for the first time in months.

Inside, the hearth glowed orange and welcoming. His siblings swarmed him, tugging at his coat, firing questions so rapidly he could barely finish a single answer. For a few precious minutes, he was neither sailor nor haunted soul; he was simply Homer.

Just son. Brother. Man.

Then the laughter dimmed. A shadow filled the doorway.

Captain Marcus stood broad-shouldered and still as a mast, eyes flicking between pride and restraint. The warmth of the room paused.

He stepped forward, boots heavy on the floorboards, and extended a hard, formal hand. Homer took it, feeling the familiar callouses. The handshake lingered with the resonance of question more than greeting.

Then Marcus's second hand rose, hesitated, and rested on Homer's shoulder. Rough, trembling slightly. The weight of it broke something inside Homer. His chest caved inward, breath catching high in his throat. When Marcus drew him into an embrace, Homer's muscles gave way, breath escaping in a soft, shaking exhale. Whale oil and salt clung to the old coat.

Like the return of a prodigal son, it was the closest thing to forgiveness he had ever known: the quiet recognition that wandering, regret, and distance did not disqualify him from being welcomed back. No reckoning followed, no conditions were set. He was simply received, because love had outlasted the absence.

That night, over bowls of chowder, they spoke in measured tones. Marcus asked about the voyage, the Navy, storms, men, losses but never about fear or loneliness. Beneath their surface words, another conversation rippled: longing, unspoken hurts, a love too proud to name.

When the others slept, the two men remained beside the warmth. The silence between them was no longer hostile, only tired, worn like an old sail left to dry. Marcus stared into the flames, jaw working as though the words were heavy. He rubbed his hands together once, slow and deliberate, as if warming them against a cold he could not shake.

"You were born into a world I wasn't ready for," he said at last, voice low, rough as the timbers of an old ship. "I wasn't fit to be a father. Hell, I thought… it'd be better if you hadn't come along. Not because I didn't want you, rather because I didn't know how."

The confession struck Homer like cold surf. But he stayed still, watching regret carve deeper lines into the man's face.

Marcus drew a slow breath, his hands clasped between his knees. "When you turned away from the family trade of whaling, I took it as betrayal. The sea was all I'd ever known, all my father gave me. I thought keeping the Deep name tied to the ships was the only way to honor what came before. When you walked away, I didn't see your courage. Only my failure." He shook his head and said, "I didn't know how to love a son who didn't want the life that made me. Rather than speak with you, I spoke at you… with criticism, command. It was the only language I knew."

He looked up then, eyes dulled by the fire's dying glow.

"You didn't abandon me, Homer. You just found a world I couldn't follow you into. I see that now."

Marcus opened his mouth as if to say more, then closed it again. Whatever followed seemed to lose its shape before reaching his tongue. He nodded once, accepting the space the words could not cross.

Homer waited before responding, letting the truth resonate with his soul. The fire had settled to a soft amber, flickering the faintest light over his father's face. He watched Marcus as a sailor studies the sea after a storm while still unsettled, but honest.

Then Homer leaned forward placing his elbows on his knees and spoke with a reverence deeper than pride. "I think I finally see it. You gave me the sea with its moods, its dangers, its grace. Even when I tried to run from it, it called me back. We both followed the same tide, just in different ways."

Marcus's sternness wavered, the firelight softening him. He looked up, a faint flicker in his eyes revealed something, maybe surprise or maybe relief. Homer continued, voice soft but sure.

"We're not so different, you and I. You hunted what you loved because it was the only way you knew how to live. I served it because it was the only escape I found that kept me in the tides while retaining sovereignty. The sea shaped us both. It gave us something shared even when we didn't know how to share anything else. And maybe that's enough. Maybe that's something to celebrate."

The old man's mouth twitched, a movement caught somewhere between a grimace and a smile. The logs settled with a sigh, sending up one last curl of smoke that rose like a small flag of truce. For the first time, Homer didn't feel the need to fix anything, to prove or defend. He simply sat there beside his father, two men joined by tide and blood, letting the silence speak what words could not. He rubbed his palms together, warming them by the dying fire before speaking.

"When I was in port after the Pawnee accident," Homer continued, "I met a man named Dr. Charles Young. A… sort of scholar of the mind, I guess you'd call him. Not the kind you'd see in a sickbay, but the kind who helps a man understand what storms he's carrying on the inside."

Marcus grunted softly, not in dismissal but in caution, as though waiting to see if this conversation would drift into waters he had no charts for. Homer noticed and adjusted his tone.

"I won't bore you with the deeper pieces," he said gently. "I know that's not your way. But he helped me see something important. Something about myself… and something about us."

Marcus's jaw tightened, but he didn't look away. Homer took that as permission to continue.

"I learned that the dreams I kept having were parts of myself fighting. Parts I didn't understand. Dr. Young said every man carries those fights. The things we fear. The things we're ashamed of. The things we don't talk about." He paused. "I think you've carried some of those too. And maybe no one ever gave you the words for them."

Marcus shifted uncomfortable, but listening.

"I'm not asking for you to change into someone you're not, Father. I know you feel things deeply too, more than you let on. And I know the world you come from didn't teach you how to say those things out loud. But Dr. Young helped me see that we both followed the sea for the same reason. It's where we knew how to breathe."

Marcus stared into the embers, throat tight.

"So when I try to talk to you about what I learned," Homer said, "I'm not trying to pull you into strange ideas. I'm just trying to bridge the gap between us. I want you to know the man I'm becoming, and I want to know the man you've always been... even the parts you never speak about. I've never wanted to stand above you, Father. Only beside you. Just to be your son... and to be seen by you. That's all I've ever wanted."

A long silence followed. Outside, the wind leaned against the shutters. Marcus's eyes flickered with pain, pride, and something softer he tried to hide.

"I'm no good with that mind-talk," Marcus muttered, almost apologetic. "But... I hear you, boy. More than you know. You're a better man than I gave you credit for," Marcus said finally, voice scraping with truth.

Homer accepted the words with quiet reverence, as though receiving sacrament, not as praise but as something consecrated by time and struggle. They moved through him slowly, settling into places long held tight, easing a tension he had carried since boyhood. In that moment, he understood how deeply he had waited to be seen in this way, and how carefully he would carry what had finally been given.

They lingered for a quiet moment longer before Marcus suggested settling down to rest for the evening. Marcus offered the final nod, and Homer returned it with a solemn smile. Left alone, Homer felt the night pressing gently around him as he finally lay down, soothed by the sound of the tide rolling beyond the dunes. In his dreams, a finger draws two rings in the sand with one encompassing the other.

Chapter Thirty-Three

"Love Unfurled"

Homer awoke before dawn, drawing deep, steady breaths of gratitude, feeling a lightness in his chest he had not known in years. The air in the room felt calm and expectant, as though the morning itself were waiting with him. Fragments of his dream lingered at the edge of his awareness, and he found himself returning again and again to the image of the circles traced in sand, wondering what they might be asking him to notice.

He reached for his journal while the memory was still warm, careful not to disturb its fragile clarity. His hand moved quickly across the page as he wrote down what he could recall, then paused to sketch a circle, and within it another. The act felt instinctive rather than deliberate. Though the image was simple, it stirred layers of thought and feeling that reached beyond words, calling up impressions of continuity, connection, and quiet resolve.

He watched the shapes take form, his eyes following the smooth lines as he fully woke. There was something steady and reassuring in their balance, something that eased his breathing and settled his mind. The circles seemed to rest together in a shared center, offering a sense of order that did not demand explanation. Before closing the journal, Homer added one final line, pressing the words into the page with care, as if sealing a truth he had carried for a long time: "The chain was broken."

Rather than marking an end, perhaps it was a signal of new beginnings. Noko's laughter drifted through his memory like sunlight over water, warming him from within. He smiled at the thought of her, letting her presence fill the quiet room. "I should make my way to the beach for an early morning walk, to greet the rising sun," he thought, dressing warmly to meet the brisk ocean air.

The first morning light stretched across the dunes, painting the sand in pale gold and the surf in liquid silver. Homer walked along the familiar stretch of beach, the obsidian stone he had left the day before atop the small cairn was absent. Noko was there, standing near the water's edge, her gaze tracing the horizon. She turned as he approached, and her smile, warm and unwavering, made the time at sea feel both distant and inconsequential.

"Homer," she said, her voice trembling with joy, letting the single word unfold between them. It carried welcome and relief, recognition born of long remembering. She spoke his name as one speaks something precious aloud, confirming it was real, while honoring what had endured. At that moment, Homer understood that he had been awaited with faith and love.

He knelt before her, the sand cool beneath his knees, and gently reached for her hand as though approaching something both familiar and newly precious. She did not pull away. When she opened her palm, he saw the obsidian stone resting there, the same one he had carried across oceans and through nights of doubt, now returned to him as if it had never truly left her keeping. It lay quietly against her skin, patient and unassuming, as though it had been waiting all along for this precise convergence of time and place.

"I'm home," he said softly.

The words surprised him in their simplicity. They carried more than arrival. They held years of longing swallowed back, of losses borne without witness, of fear survived and faith rebuilt in fragments. They carried the stubborn will that had kept him breathing when surrender would have been easier, and the quiet hope that somewhere beyond the horizon, this moment had been forming without his knowing.

Noko's eyes softened as she looked at him, shimmering with a tenderness he remembered from boyhood, yet now deepened by time and patience. It was the same gaze that had once followed him down familiar paths, now steady enough to meet him where he stood. "I've waited for you," she said, her voice gentle and sure. "And you've come back. Stronger. Wiser. Still here."

She closed her fingers around his, drawing his hand into hers. The stone was pressed between their palms, cool at first, then warming as their skin met, binding what had been carried apart into a single shared presence. In that quiet contact, Homer felt the past loosen its grip, not erased, but accepted. What had been endured no longer stood between them. It rested there with them, held and understood, as the tide continued its steady rhythm just beyond their feet.

Homer exhaled slowly, letting the salt-tinged air move through him and settle where tension had long made its home. The beach opened around them in a wide, receptive calm. The ocean rolled in with steady resolve, its waves arriving and retreating without insistence, while the distant cries of gulls passed overhead like loose threads in the morning sky. Nothing asked anything of him. Nothing waited to be satisfied.

The familiar elements gathered quietly, shaping the moment

into something that felt safe rather than exposed. Sand pressed firm beneath his boots. The horizon held its line. Even the wind seemed to soften as it crossed the shore. It was as if the world had arranged itself to receive whatever might be spoken next, without judgment or consequence.

In that ease, Homer sensed a change within himself. He could speak here without measuring his words, without standing at attention to memory or expectation. No command hovered nearby. No duty tightened its grip. The weight he had carried so long loosened, and the words he held did not rush forward or retreat. They simply waited, ready to be shared in their own time.

"I have to tell you something," he began, his voice low, as though the words needed to be kept close. "About the ship. About the explosion. About Robert." His fingers tightened reflexively, the memory passing through him before he could stop it. "The blast took him. Took others too. I was trapped below, swallowed by smoke and darkness, and for a while I was certain that was where it would end."

He paused, drawing a careful breath. "I didn't think I would survive it. Not the fire, not what came after. I wrestled with despair, with guilt I didn't know how to carry. And when it all became too much, when I reached the edge of myself, I went overboard."

Her hand found his, warm and steady, and she did not let go. Noko listened as Homer spoke, not interrupting, not steering the telling, only staying with him as the words emerged in their own uneven rhythm. He shared the wounds he had carried inward for so long, the moments of fear, guilt, and wonder, and she received them without flinching, as though there were nothing about him that required correction or defense.

Time loosened its hold as he spoke. The light shifted across the sand, the tide advanced and withdrew, and still they remained there, tracing the shape of his life together. They moved through moments of joy and loss, of hope and despair, each memory unfolding into the next without urgency or tally. What mattered was the telling itself, and the quiet certainty that he was no longer carrying these things alone.

"And then the whales came," he said quietly, the words arriving with a reverence that surprised him. "A whole pod. They moved around me, close enough that I could feel the water change, like the sea itself had shifted its attention." His eyes lifted as if the memory were unfolding again before him. "They guided me. Kept me afloat. Brought me back."

He shook his head slightly, searching for language that would not cheapen what he had felt. "I don't know how I would have lived otherwise. I know that much. Out there, I wasn't alone anymore. It felt like being gathered into something living and aware, a kind of belonging I had never known." His voice softened. "Not something I can explain well. Only something I can carry. Something that stayed with me."

Noko did not look away. She tightened her grip on his hand, her gaze steady and sure. When he finished, she exhaled softly, as though she had been holding her breath with him.

"Maybe you were never meant to carry it alone," she said. "Some things come to meet us when we can't reach any farther. They found you when you needed them. And now you're here."

He looked at her then, his voice lowering, as though the words belonged to a quieter register. "I met someone while I was away," he said. "A gentleman. A doctor of the mind." He hesitated, searching for language that would not flatten the experience. "He helped me understand the dreams I was having. He showed me they weren't warnings or omens, but the quiet parts of me asking to be seen. Old places. Parts of myself that had been there all along, carrying more than I knew how to name."

Homer paused, drawing a careful breath, letting the moment settle before continuing. "But through all of it," he said softly, almost reverently, "I kept writing you letters I never sent. I turned every thought over, examined every feeling I could reach." He opened his palm, revealing the smooth black stone resting there. "And this stayed with me. It never left."

He looked at the stone for a moment, then back at her. "It kept your memory alive when everything else felt uncertain. Every day, it reminded me of you. Of home. Of the life I was trying to find my way back to."

Noko reached for his hand, her fingers warm and familiar against his. She held it with a steadiness that felt practiced, as though she had been doing so all along in quieter ways.

"I felt it, Homer," she said. "Every letter you didn't send. Every thought you carried through the dark." Her thumb brushed lightly against his knuckles, once, then stilled. "I didn't always know how or when, but I knew you were still there. Still reaching."

She met his gaze without hesitation. "So I waited, without doubt or fear." A small, warming smile touched her lips. "I waited because I believed you would come back. And you did."

Homer's eyes softened as he looked at her, the weight of the moment settling into his chest. "I thought I had lost you forever," he said quietly. "I carried that fear with me longer than I care to admit."

His gaze searched her face, as if confirming she was truly there. "And now here you are."

He drew a breath, but the words he reached for would not come cleanly. His voice faltered, the sentence slipping from his grasp. He shook his head slightly, a small, helpless smile breaking through. What he felt could not be shaped quickly enough to be spoken, and he let the silence hold what his voice could not.

"You don't have to begin," Noko whispered, a gentle smile touching her lips. "There's nothing to catch up on." Her thumb traced a small, absent circle against his hand. "We step forward from here. The moments we missed, the mornings we didn't see together, they're not lost. They're waiting for us now."

Noko's gaze drifted toward the ocean, following the long line where water met sky. She did not speak right away. When she did, her voice carried the calm of something remembered rather than taught.

"The whales," she said softly. "The water. They have their own ways of knowing." She paused, as if choosing words that belonged to the place rather than to explanation. "In my people's stories, whales are not just animals. They are relatives. Keepers of memory. They move between worlds we don't always see."

She looked back at him then. "They came to you because they recognized you. Because you were listening, even when you didn't know you were. Nothing pulled them. Nothing ordered them. They answered."

Her hand tightened gently around his. "Your life mattered in that moment. It still does. And the sea knew it."

Homer felt the tension in his chest ease, the sharp edge of fear giving way to something steadier. “So all of this,” he said quietly, “my survival… it wasn’t just luck.”

Noko squeezed his hand, her touch firm and reassuring. “No,” she said. “It came from being seen.” Her gaze returned briefly to the water before meeting his again. “By the sea. By those who move within it. By the life that kept answering you when you didn’t know how to answer yourself.”

She smiled softly. “You were never as alone as you thought.”

He leaned forward until the space between them disappeared, resting his forehead gently against hers. The warmth of her skin steadied him, anchoring him more surely than words ever could. “I don’t know how to thank you,” he softly whispered. “For understanding. For staying. For being here when I finally found my way back.”

The words felt small compared to what he carried, but she did not seem to need more. In that closeness, gratitude no longer asked to be spoken perfectly. It simply existed, shared in breath and stillness.

“You don’t need words,” she whispered. “Just this.” She pressed her forehead more firmly against his, as if to anchor him. “Trust that being here matters. We’ll carry what’s come before with care, and we’ll do it the only way that makes sense.” A pause. “Side by side.”

For a long while, they stood together in easy silence, the surf rising and retreating at their feet, the morning light catching briefly on the obsidian stone before slipping away again. Around them, the beach carried on in its familiar rhythms, steady and unchanged. The life of ships, storms, duty, and sorrow settled behind him, no longer pressing for his attention, no longer demanding to be carried forward in the same way.

What lay ahead took shape quietly. It was a life informed by what he had endured and steadied by who now stood beside him, one shaped through patience, presence, and shared breath. Homer felt the difference in his body, in the way his shoulders eased and his breath found a natural pace. Whatever came next would be built slowly, with care, and in the company of those who mattered most.

The morning lingered longer than either of them expected. They walked the shoreline together, neither in a hurry, letting the tide set the rhythm. When they reached the narrow path that bent away from the dunes toward town, Noko slowed. She brushed the sand from her hands and looked once more toward the water, as if offering a silent acknowledgment to whatever had carried him back.

They did not say goodbye in words. She pressed her forehead briefly to his, a gesture familiar from years ago, then stepped back with a calm certainty that needed no promise attached to it. Homer watched her walk the length of the beach until the curve of the shore softened her outline and the light folded her into the distance. He felt no ache in watching her go, only a quiet assurance that separation no longer meant absence.

The path home wound through tall grass and weathered fences, the earth still cool beneath his boots. As he walked, the world felt newly dimensional, as though every sound and texture had been returned to him with greater clarity. The cry of gulls overhead, the distant knock of halyards against masts, the steady pulse of the sea moving in and out of his awareness like breath. Nothing demanded explanation. Nothing needed to be held too tightly.

By the time the cottage came into view, the day had begun to soften, light settling gently against the clapboard walls. His mother met him at the door as though she had sensed his approach, her arms opening before he could speak. He stepped into her embrace and felt something long held loosen in his chest. She smelled of cedar smoke and bread dough, of all the small, steady labors that had shaped his life before the sea ever claimed him. Her hand pressed firmly between his shoulders, not as reassurance but as recognition, and he allowed himself to be held without reserve.

Inside, the house breathed with familiar life. Voices moved from room to room, low and easy, punctuated by laughter and the clink of dishes. The hearth glowed, casting warmth that reached deeper than skin. Homer stood for a moment simply taking it in. The rhythm of family. The comfort of shared space. The quiet miracle of being known without explanation. Here, he did not need to account for who he had become or what he carried. He was home, and that was enough.

Later that evening, when the house had settled and the sounds of the day had softened into rest, Homer unpacked his journal and sat at the table beneath the lamplight. The room held him gently as he began to write, the presence of his family lingering like a steady current beneath his thoughts:

"I find courage in the strength of the sails tempered with the demands of an otherwise unforgiving sea. Similarly, in the footsteps of the men I respect, I see the shape of who I wish to become; strong, honorable, yet powerfully humble. To surrender is to know the power love deeply holds, for love conquers fears through such strategic measure."

Epilogue

Long after everything had quieted, after life resumed its familiar shape, the dream continued to move through me.

The first emotion that greeted me upon waking was beauty. The underwater world I had inhabited felt crisp and alive, rendered with a clarity that lingered even as my eyes opened to morning light. I had moved through it as a whale, my body sleek and powerful, guided by instinct rather than effort. Each motion carried a sense of belonging, as though my skin itself understood its purpose, cutting cleanly through the water without resistance.

What surprised me most was not the clarity of the images, but the clarity of sensation. I felt invigorated, alert, and deeply at ease, as though my form itself understood something my waking mind was still learning. There was no sense of strain or separation. My skin, thick and smooth, parted the water as though it had been shaped for that purpose alone. The ocean did not resist me. It received me.

The closest comparison I could find was from childhood, when I used to dream of flying. In those dreams, I would rise effortlessly, drifting above rooftops and trees, free from gravity and fear. The air itself seemed to hold me aloft and the world unfolded beneath me without boundary. I remember the disappointment of waking, the dull return to limitation. This was different. The memory of the whale did not fade with consciousness. It followed me into waking life, intact and insistent, as though it had not been a dream at all but a remembered state.

I had heard it said that dreams occupy only fleeting moments of the night, fragments stitched together by the mind. Yet this experience unfolded with patience and coherence. Time moved differently there. The surroundings were rich with detail, and the emotions they evoked arrived gently, with depth and continuity. It felt less like a passing vision and more like a story allowed to complete itself. Even after waking, it continued to surface in my thoughts, reappearing during quiet moments when my breath slowed and my attention softened.

I began to understand the importance of those moments of drifting awareness. For much of my life, daydreaming had been treated as a fault, a lapse in discipline or focus. I remembered being corrected for it as a child, urged to remain present in the narrow sense defined by others. Now I see it differently. Those moments of inward wandering were not an escape, but an opening. A way of listening. In stillness, the imagination does not escape reality; it engages it more deeply. It is there that connections emerge, unforced and unannounced.

That inward listening led me to reflect more deeply on the bond between humans, animals, and the world that holds us all. I began to sense that the damage inflicted upon the natural world does not end at the surface. It moves inward, embedding itself in bodies, behaviors, and inherited patterns. Just as human trauma can echo across generations, shaping lives long after the initial wound, so too might the suffering of animals leave traces that persist beyond the moment of harm.

The study of epigenetics suggests that experience alters expression, that memory is not confined to thought alone but carried within the body itself. I found myself wondering whether the same principle applied beyond our species. Whether pain endured by creatures of land and sea might be woven into their very being, carried forward as a silent inheritance. Perhaps the bonds of matter, the same carbon structures that link all life, hold more than form. Perhaps they hold memories.

As these reflections deepened, I realized that understanding the precise origin of my dream mattered less than attending to what it had revealed. The dream had been an opening, not a conclusion. It invited me to consider how closely our inner lives mirror the world we shape, and how neglect, consumption, and disregard fracture both landscapes at once. In recognizing that connection, I felt an invitation toward responsibility, kinship, and ethical husbandry.

Our dreams, I came to believe, are not merely messages delivered to us. They are questions posed quietly, asking whether we are willing to listen. In the stillness of sleep, the body restores itself, and the mind loosens its grip on certainty. What emerges in that space often carries truths we are too hurried to receive by day.

I remembered a line that had once come to me in another dream, words that had stayed with me longer than I understood at the time:

"If you don't remember what caused you to sin, you are fast on your way to repeating sin again!"

To sin is not necessarily to act in malice, but to fall out of alignment. The Hebrew root translates as "to miss the mark," a term borrowed from archery that describes a deviation in direction rather than a moral failure. Understood this way, sin becomes less about condemnation and more about course correction. It invites awareness, not punishment, and offers the possibility of returning to a truer aim.

I imagined memory not as something stored solely in minds, but as something vast and enduring, a kind of cosmic record carried in patterns too small and too large for us to measure. Perhaps intelligence itself moves through creation in this way, remembering through us, urging recalibration when we drift too far from balance.

I once believed that becoming whole meant arriving somewhere final. Now I understand that wholeness is a practice, renewed each time we choose awareness over habit. The sea taught me that. So did the land. And somewhere between them, I sense another crossing waiting.

And so I listen.

Because some journeys do not announce their next passage. Whatever I once was, and whatever I became, are not finished speaking to one another. The sea remembers.

And so, it seems, do I.

Author's Note

I did not write this book to offer certainty. I wrote it to explore what happens when we listen more closely to dreams, to memory, and to the stories we inherit through our bodies and our world. The sea has always been both literal and symbolic to me, a place of danger, transformation, and belonging.

This story does not ask to be interpreted so much as experienced. If it lingers, if it raises questions rather than resolves them, then it has done what it was meant to do. Like the sea, some stories are not meant to be mastered or explained. They are meant to be listened to.

Acknowledgements

This book owes its existence to many visible and unseen influences, and I am grateful for the currents that carried it into being.

Foremost, I wish to acknowledge Herman Melville, whose Moby-Dick continues to echo across literature and consciousness alike. His work deeply inspired this story, opening a door through which generations of writers have passed, inviting us to grapple with the vastness of the sea, the mystery of obsession, and the fragile humanity that sails between them. Any conversation this book holds with whales, with fate, or with the inner lives of sailors and the lifestyle onboard a whaling ship, is made possible by his enduring vision.

In shaping this work, I was influenced by thinkers and teachers who approached inner life with curiosity rather than certainty. The writings of Carl Jung helped me understand dreams, symbols, and inherited memory as living processes. His voice along with many others, whether scientific, mythic, or poetic, informed this work in ways both direct and subtle.

To those who listened as this story found its voice, who offered patience, insight, and encouragement along the way, I offer a humble thank you.

Finally, to the readers who bring their own attention, curiosity, and care to these pages, may you find something here that speaks back to you.

A Note to the Reader

The foundation of this book rests in dreams, reflections, and moments of inward listening. If you find yourself stirred by a dream of your own while reading, you may wish to write it down before it fades. Some dreams ask only to be witnessed. Others seem to want company. If you ever feel called to share one, I would be honored to receive it. Like the sea, these experiences do not belong to any one of us alone.

About the Author

Daniel Miller is a U.S. Navy veteran who served as a Hospital Corpsman with the Fleet Marine Forces during Operation Enduring Freedom, completing one deployment with 2nd Battalion, 3rd Marines on Unit Deployment Program rotation in 2010. His experiences at sea and in combat medicine shaped his understanding of trauma, resilience, and the ways meaning is carried through the body long after events have passed.

In addition to his military service, Daniel has worked as a missionary and police officer. He is the founder of Operation Freedom Recovery, a nonprofit organization and podcast dedicated to supporting military veterans and their families through recovery and reintegration. His work centers on exploring pathways to healing that honor lived experience, personal agency, and inner transformation.

Daniel is a certified breathwork facilitator and has worked with individuals navigating trauma, transition, and identity, helping them reconnect with presence and embodied awareness. He completed his MBA, integrating his background in service and wellness with systems thinking and leadership.

His writing emerges from the intersection of lived experience, imagination, and careful listening, often exploring themes of memory, inheritance, and the relationship between human life and the natural world.

He lives in Idaho with his family and is a proud father.

www.ingramcontent.com/pod-product-compliance
Lightning Source LLC
LaVergne TN
LVHW020713110826
845149LV00012B/2235

* 9 7 8 1 9 6 8 1 4 9 2 4 6 *